Work without Jobs

Management on the Cutting Edge

Robert J. Holland Jr., series editor

Published in cooperation with *MIT Sloan Management Review*

The AI Advantage: How to Put the Artificial Intelligence Revolution to Work
Thomas H. Davenport

The Technology Fallacy: How People Are the Real Key to Digital Transformation
Gerald C. Kane, Anh Nguyen Phillips, Jonathan Copulsky, and Garth Andrus

Designed for Digital: How to Architect Your Business for Sustained Success
Jeanne W. Ross, Cynthia Beath, and Martin Mocker

See Sooner, Act Faster: How Vigilant Leaders Thrive in an Era of Digital Turbulence
George S. Day and Paul J. H. Schoemaker

Leading in the Digital World: How to Foster Creativity, Collaboration, and Inclusivity
Amit S. Mukherjee

The Ends Game: How Smart Companies Stop Selling Products and Start Delivering Value
Marco Bertini and Oded Koenigsberg

Open Strategy: Mastering Disruption from Outside the C-Suite
Christian Stadler, Julia Hautz, Kurt Matzler, and Stephan Friedrich von den Eichen

The Transformation Myth: Leading Your Organization through Uncertain Times
Gerald C. Kane, Rich Nanda, Anh Nguyen Phillips, and Jonathan R. Copulsky

Winning the Right Game: How to Disrupt, Defend, and Deliver in a Changing World
Ron Adner

The Digital Multinational: Navigating the New Normal in Global Business
Satish Nambisan and Yadong Luo

Work without Jobs: How to Reboot Your Organization's Work Operating System
Ravin Jesuthasan and John W. Boudreau

Work without Jobs

How to Reboot Your Organization's
Work Operating System

Ravin Jesuthasan and John W. Boudreau

The MIT Press
Cambridge, Massachusetts
London, England

The MIT Press would like to thank the anonymous peer reviewers who provided comments on drafts of this book. The generous work of academic experts is essential for establishing the authority and quality of our publications. We acknowledge with gratitude the contributions of these otherwise uncredited readers.

This book was set in Stone Serif and Stone Sans by Westchester Publishing Services. Printed and bound in the United States of America.

Library of Congress Cataloging-in-Publication Data

Names: Jesuthasan, Ravin, 1968– author. | Boudreau, John W., author.
Title: Work without jobs : how to reboot your organization's work operating system / Ravin Jesuthasan and John W. Boudreau.
Description: Cambridge, Massachusetts : The MIT Press, 2022. |
    Series: Management on the cutting edge | Includes bibliographical references and index.
Identifiers: LCCN 2021031217 | ISBN 9780262046411 (hardcover)
Subjects: LCSH: Organizational change. | Work--Technological innovations. |
    Personnel management--Technological innovations. | Flexible work arrangements. | Automation.
Classification: LCC HD58.8 .J478 2022 | DDC 658.4/02--dc23
LC record available at https://lccn.loc.gov/2021031217

10 9 8 7 6 5 4 3 2 1

Contents

Series Foreword

The world does not lack for management ideas. Thousands of researchers, practitioners, and other experts produce tens of thousands of articles, books, papers, posts, and podcasts each year. But only a scant few promise to truly move the needle on practice, and fewer still dare to reach into the future of what management will become. It is this rare breed of idea—meaningful to practice, grounded in evidence, and *built for the future*—that we seek to present in this series.

Robert J. Holland Jr.

Managing Director
MIT Sloan Management Review

Introduction: Work without Jobs Is the New Work Operating System

Here's a brainteaser: you are given a candle, a box of tacks, and a book of matches. How do you attach the candle to a wall so that it can be lit without dripping wax onto the floor below? The solution is to deconstruct the box of tacks into its parts (box, tacks), attach the box to the wall with the tacks, and attach the candle to the bottom of the box. In experiments, people who get the tacks inside the box can't solve the problem, but those given a pile of tacks beside the box solve it easily.

Typically, work is "constructed" into job descriptions similar to the box of tacks; the descriptions become a repository of competencies, performance indicators, and reward packages. This obscures powerful opportunities to optimize your workforce's productivity, alignment, and engagement. Tapping those opportunities requires "deconstruction" and "reconstruction," a vital emerging capability for organizations. Deconstruction means reconsidering jobs to see the underlying components such as tasks, projects, and so on, and it means reconsidering jobholders in terms of their capabilities and skills. Reconstruction means reassembling the components differently, into new and more optimal combinations that are not limited only to new jobs and jobholders. It's like the brainteaser. The box and the tacks are reassembled into a more useful combination than the original "box that contains tacks." In the new work operating system, this deconstruction and reconstruction happens perpetually, offering organizations, leaders, and workers far more options. It also requires fundamentally rethinking concepts like work, leadership, culture, and organization.

In the dynamic work environments of the future, organization dilemmas closely resemble the candle puzzle. It's time to take the tacks out of the box.

Understanding and effectively responding to the future of work will increasingly require this kind of deconstruction and reconstruction. You can already see this when work automation (such as artificial intelligence (AI) and robots) and alternative work arrangements (such as "gigs") present opportunities that are not easily solved with the existing job definitions. Only at the work elements level can you uncover the key building blocks to understanding and optimizing this future work world.

The New Work Operating System

This book describes why and how the future of work will increasingly rest on the granular or "deconstructed" elements of jobs (tasks, projects, etc.) and workers (skills, capabilities, etc.). We call this the "new work operating system."

Think of an operating system on a computer, tablet, or mobile phone. The operating system is the software that communicates with the hardware and allows other programs to run. Within the operating system are fundamental choices about the protocols and connecting elements. Think of how differently devices running Apple's iOS system function compared to devices running Microsoft's Windows OS. On one device you swipe and on the other you click. These protocols eventually fade into the background and are hardly noticed or questioned. Yet they become glaringly obvious when external software programs are not compatible with both operating systems, requiring two different versions, one for each device.

In the same way, a *work* operating system is the basic system that allows for work engagements and connects outside programs to the organization's work system.

The traditional work operating system encapsulates work into jobs and workers into jobholders through an employment relationship. Like the operating system on a computer or phone, a work operating system imposes certain requirements about how work relationships will operate.

Job titles, job hierarchies, and job qualifications become the accepted language of work. External connections, such as education programs, social policy, unions, and so on, learn to connect with the operating system by tailoring their interactions to the jobs that are the unit of work. Society talks of "good jobs." Worker voice is described as "unions for employees." The work experience is framed as the "employee experience" or the "employment value proposition." This traditional job-based operating system is so ubiquitous that it fades into the background, yet it becomes glaringly obvious when new challenges emerge.

For example, work automation seldom replaces an entire job. Instead, it replaces some of the tasks in a job, but the rest are still done by humans. If the human is now doing 80 percent of the tasks in the "job" but automation does the other 20 percent, how do you define the job? This gets even trickier if the human is now 50 percent more productive, doing 80 percent of the tasks of their job. What do you pay them? You can only find answers if you reconsider the situation in terms of the deconstructed job tasks, and you realize that automation will require perpetually deconstructing and reconstructing the work.

This book proposes that accelerated change, demands for organizational agility, work automation, efforts to increase diversity and equity, and emerging alternative work arrangements are rapidly revealing that the traditional work operating system based on jobs and jobholders is too cumbersome and ill-suited to the future. We propose and describe a new work operating system that deconstructs jobs into their components and allows work to be perpetually reinvented by recombining those more granular elements. This means that work systems (e.g., planning, sourcing, choosing, assigning, developing, engaging, rewarding) must evolve to reflect this new language of work. The cases we describe will illustrate how leading organizations are embracing work deconstruction and reinvention, at the cutting edge of work automation and worker engagement, and how they are building and implementing this new operating system, revealing the future of work.

After reading this book, leaders will understand—and be more prepared to successfully address—emerging issues like automation, AI and robotics, the gig economy, and the future of work. We will show how this new work operating system can be implemented using well-grounded and practical approaches that transform how they plan for, acquire, deploy, develop, and manage their investment in their workforces and work options. However, unlike typical approaches that take the job-based work operating system as a given, we show how true solutions require rethinking this fundamental assumption.

Work automation only rarely involves substituting a robot, chatbot, or AI for the human worker in a particular job. Rather, most work automation effects will reinvent the work, requiring that humans and automation work together, as some of the tasks formerly done by the human worker are now done by automation but many of the formerly human tasks will still be done by the human worker. For example, the traditional job of infrastructure inspector/repairperson for things like power lines or pipelines combines in a single job tasks such as physically inspecting, recording data, diagnosing potential faults, and repairing the faults. Increasingly, the new work combines humans with automated drones or sensors that take on the tasks of physical inspection and recording data, leaving the human workers to focus on diagnosis and creative repair solutions, with the repairs carried out by remotely guided automated machines. Such reinvented work is impossible to conceive if approached by asking "how many of our inspectors/repairpersons will be replaced by automation," but it is easily conceived if the job is deconstructed and each task is optimized to be done by a human or by automation.

Similarly, "alternative work arrangements" beyond regular full-time employment (such as contractors, freelancers, and volunteers) seldom fully substitute a nonemployee for an employee. Rather, some of the tasks in a job formerly done by a regular employee might be done by a contractor or freelancer, but many of the remaining job tasks should still be done by a regular employee. Consider the work of a bank teller or retail associate, for example. The traditional job assumes that a human worker will be on site carrying out tasks ranging from helping customers to stocking shelves to recording transactions and inventory. Cloud technology enabled some tasks to be done remotely, such as advising online shoppers, offering descriptions of banking services, handling customer complaints and returns, and analyzing customer data for patterns to improve products or services. If the work can be done from home, then workers can be engaged through a remote platform.

However, the job tasks that have been shifted to remote work are only a subset of the tasks in the formerly in-person job. The retail stores and banks still need in-person associates to do tasks such as assisting store customers and providing in-person transactions. As some tasks shift to remote work, the in-person associates can focus more on providing a compelling in-person customer experience, now drawing on the cloud data that better personalizes that in-person experience. Taking this a step further, the remote work tasks might be done by workers who are engaged not as employees but instead on a freelance platform. As with work automation, these challenges reveal that some of the work tasks formerly contained in the regular full-time job of an in-person customer associate will now be done by workers engaged with alternative arrangements.

The traditional work operating system similarly bundles worker capabilities into fixed units because workers in the traditional work system are "jobholders." Their skills and capabilities are matched to jobs as they enter, and it is a series of jobs that define their careers. While many organizations have "competency" systems that articulate capabilities at a more granular level, even these competency systems are used primarily to determine workers' fit for future jobs, laid out in a relatively stable sequence. The traditional work system similarly considers worker education in bundles called "degrees" or "certificates," attempting to match degrees with jobs. These traditional approaches are under increasing scrutiny as change accelerates and workers and organizations demand and expect greater agility. For example, colleges work to unbundle their offerings so that the deconstructed capabilities that comprise a college degree are more visible to hiring organizations, and they then to match those deconstructed capabilities to the work demands of companies. However, even here, the goal is to qualify students to become jobholders in the jobs of the companies. This creates significant challenges when the jobs themselves are changing. The answer lies in the new work operating system that we propose, which allows deconstructed worker capabilities to be matched to deconstructed work tasks.

Within organizations, internal talent marketplaces, sometimes called "inside gigs,"[1] challenge the idea that a worker must be confined to one job at a time. These internal platforms deconstruct jobs into tasks or projects and then make those deconstructed elements available to workers. The workers often take on a project or task in addition to their regular job to demonstrate capabilities that are not obvious in their job, to connect with a project or team that is not directly relevant to their job, or to contribute to a company mission that does not directly relate to their jobs. These platforms do more than deconstruct the job because they also track the worker capabilities and skills used in the projects or tasks and offer the workers insights as to the capabilities and skills needed to take on new projects or tasks. Thus, such internal talent marketplaces "deconstruct" the idea of a monolithic worker into granular skills and capabilities, some of which are used in their job but many others that are now visible to the organization and available for the deconstructed work on the platform.

Some may find the phrase "deconstructed worker" to conjure images of workers as mere collections of capabilities, a dehumanizing image. Another frequently used term is "fluid" work and fluid workers. One editor reacted to the phrase "fluid worker" as also dehumanizing, concerned that readers would conjure a disturbing image from the movie *The Wizard of Oz*, when the Wicked Witch of the West dissolves when doused with water. However, the new work operating system can actually enable just the opposite—a *more* human work engagement. Such systems can reveal and tap worker capabilities that were previously invisible because they weren't relevant to a current or future job. In revealing and tapping these invisible capabilities, it is now possible to engage the "whole person." For example, in one media company, an internal talent marketplace allowed an accountant to land a role providing the voiceover narration for the trailer to an upcoming film. In the traditional job-based system, the accountant's hidden capability would be invisible. In the new system where both the deconstructed task and workers' deconstructed capabilities can be seen and matched, the accountant landed the role, bringing more of their whole person to the organization.

Why We Need a New Work Operating System: From Employment, Jobs, and Jobholders toward Platforms

In the face of a growing number of work options such as gig talent, AI, and robotics, the job will soon no longer be the primary mechanism for connecting people to work. Confining "work" into a job and worker into a jobholder forces a perspective that is incapable of illuminating and optimizing the wide variety of alternative ways to engage human workers and to combine human and automated work.

We believe that deconstruction is central to implementing many of the social policy recommendations designed to make the work relationship more seamless, efficient, equitable, and transparent. Even regular full-time employment will increasingly take on the characteristics of this new work operating system. Reformulating the fundamental unit of work from being a job and the worker as a jobholder (employee or contractor) offers insights and options that the traditional job-based system simply cannot accommodate.

Virtually all social systems are still based on the concept of work as a job and worker as an employee. Policymakers and others lament the failure of social systems to support and protect workers who are not classified as employees, producing pressure to force organizations to reclassify their workers as employees, who then have access to benefits such as employer-provided health insurance, retirement accounts or pensions, unemployment insurance when they lose their job, opportunities to form unions to bargain with the employer, and so on. Government leaders often frame labor policies or future of work solutions in terms of preserving, repatriating, or creating the good jobs of the past. But this fixation on jobs actually limits the potential of their solutions.

The new world of work is one "beyond employment."[2] If leaders want to help the global and national economies to adapt to a shifting work landscape, they must focus more on new work arrangements,[3] such as platforms. In the future, policymakers, researchers, leaders, and workers must get beyond ideas such as "displaced jobholder" to describe the evolution of work experiences and instead consider workers as something like "global freelance experts."[4]

The promise to bring back factory jobs is a sticky issue—and a temporary solution even at best. The *Economist* noted that "semi-skilled manufacturing jobs are not going to return to America, or anywhere else, because they were not simply shipped abroad. They were destroyed by new ways of boosting productivity and reducing costs which heightened the distinction between routine labor and the rest of manufacturing."[5]

The *Wall Street Journal* recently reported that a twelve-year veteran machinist at Rexnord, a manufacturing company, was asked to train replacement Mexican workers when the company decided to move its factories. The Indianapolis-based machinist told the *Journal*, "That's a real kick in the ass to be asked to train your replacement, to train the man that's going to eat your bread."[6] Yet employers need not simply lay off their American laborers just because they're relocating. The machinist at Rexnord is now a trainer. In the new operating system, we would deconstruct the job to separate training (which may require long experience) from machine operation (which can be done with less experience after training). Couldn't the machinist living in Indianapolis still earn an income and add value by training new machinists remotely? On the freelance platform Upwork, there's a job listing for a "freelance network trainer" who will deliver training through online video conferencing or Webex meetings. Why couldn't similar platforms match experienced operators in one region to train inexperienced operators in another, producing economic value for the workers and the manufacturing company?

The COVID-19 pandemic and other recent crises have reinforced the idea that an increasing amount of knowledge work may be pushed into the "gig economy,"[7] which is a poor term for a broader idea that such work will be available through platforms. Freelance platforms and the gig economy usually bring to mind examples like Uber, Lyft, and

TaskRabbit, but other platforms have already evolved to locate, match, engage, and pay workers in other occupations such as computer coders, patent lawyers, and media producers.

Such platforms are poised to respond to worker displacement, too. With all the focus on gig workers, the potential for platforms to assist more traditional workers is often overlooked. Yet, a McKinsey Global Institute report estimated that online talent platforms could increase global employment by 2.4 percent by 2025.[8] What's more, platforms could help more than 230 million workers globally reduce their job search time, both decreasing unemployment periods and introducing opportunities they otherwise would have missed. One might think of the hidden value in a more fluid work system as an element of the "intangible economy,"[9] reflecting the value available to organizations, but that does not fit easily into traditional financial measures and exists beyond the traditional organizational border.

Expanding platforms to help displaced workers will require deconstructing current jobs, expanding the language of worker capabilities and opportunities, and building a new ecosystem supported by companies, governments, stakeholders, and the HR profession. It is a formidable investment but with huge social and economic returns.

Citizens often demand that corporations, governments, and society address the hardship of work displacement, but promises to preserve or repatriate the good jobs of the past are increasingly unrealistic. Such important issues demand solutions beyond jobs, including better platforms and better systems to support the discovery, usability, and awareness of these platforms. Just as the job and jobholder concepts are insufficient to meet the market-matching needs of the changing work ecosystem, they similarly are insufficient to meet essential human needs, such as income, healthcare, collective voice, healthcare security, and retirement funds. These additional needs must be better and more efficiently attached to work that exists as deconstructed work tasks and worker capabilities.

Regarding the preparation and supply of labor, organizations, policymakers, and educators wrestle with the dilemma that traditional educational credentials, bundled into degrees, are slow to respond to the changing capability needs of the organizations that hire those degree holders. What is needed is a more flexible way to think about education and credentials that allows for more granular matching of the elements of a degree or certificate to the elements of the work. Thus, the widespread acceptance of a "skills-based" approach to creating the pathway between education and work. This approach deconstructs degrees into component skills and then envisions that learners might pursue education as a series of credentials, perhaps shifting from school to work as their credentials allow and then switching back from work to school to acquire the next granular set of skills necessary to take on a future work role. In its ultimate form, such a system no longer rests on degrees matched to jobs but on capabilities matched with deconstructed work tasks and projects. This allows education providers, students, and organizations to get beyond lamenting the difficulty of matching degrees to jobs or of adjusting degrees to job changes. Instead, the deconstructed worker skills reveal options that are simply not available when the debate is framed as degrees matched to jobs.

The Accelerated Need for a New Work Operating System

Leaders need a new operating system for work that better reflects the fluidity of work and workers and better supports organizational agility. Our last two books, *Reinventing Jobs* and *Lead the Work*, revealed that leaders, workers, and work operating systems must increasingly and perpetually deconstruct jobs and workers into more granular units such as tasks and skills/capabilities.[10]

Lead the Work showed how deconstructing work was essential to uncovering new options for sourcing, rewarding, and engaging workers, with some work elements best done by regular full-time employees and others best done by through freelancers, contractors, volunteers, and gamers or through other engagements. *Reinventing Jobs* extended these ideas to encompass work automation. Virtually every scientific study of work automation shows that only very rarely will the result be "employees in jobs replaced by automation." Instead, work automation can be optimized only by understanding how humans and automation will be *combined*. Again, work and worker deconstruction were essential to the framework that enables leaders to understand and anticipate how automation might augment or reinvent human work. Leaders trapped in the typical framework of jobs and employees will simply be unprepared even to understand work automation, let alone optimize it.

Our previous books showed the effects of work deconstruction and its ability to clarify, reveal, and optimize work solutions that reach beyond employment and incorporate combinations of humans and automation. In this book, we show how organizations can actually implement work deconstruction to reap the benefits that we described in the earlier books.

We first describe this new work operating system's principles and components. Then, we illuminate the new work system using real-world cases, drawn from our extensive fieldwork with many large global enterprises and research with leading organizations like the World Economic Forum and the Global Consortium to Reimagine HR, Employment Alternatives, Talent, and the Enterprise (CHREATE) on the future of HR. These examples will vividly illustrate how the principles and components of the new work operating system provide a unique new framework for addressing vital emerging work dilemmas. The examples also offer tangible "how to" demonstrations that will help leaders envision how the framework of principles and components of the new work operating system can be applied in practice.

Of course, as with any emerging change, "the future is unevenly distributed," to quote William Gibson. Organizations may still see much work that can be well managed using traditional work operating system where an "employee" holds a job. However, that is no excuse for ignoring this future work evolution, nor to ignore the need for work and worker deconstruction. Our fieldwork shows that the work *most* in need of the new operating system often falls at the *tipping point* where new technology arrives or new work arrangements become more optimal. When that happens, leaders realize that achieving the full potential of work and automation rests not on technological advancements but on optimizing work, and that requires a fundamentally different paradigm. As AI and robotics proliferate, this tipping point increasingly affects more organizations and more of the work within them. This book will focus on these tipping points, which will help leaders diagnose where those tipping points exist or are imminent within their organizations. Thus, this book will prepare leaders in advance for the future of work.

Work Automation Combines Human and Automated Work

Work automation is often framed in simple terms—how many jobs will new technology replace? For example, the number of bank teller jobs *increased* with the number of ATMs. In 1985, the United States had 60,000 ATMs and 485,000 bank tellers. In 2002, there were 352,000 ATMs and 527,000 bank tellers.

James Bessen explains why more ATMs spawned more teller jobs.[11] The average bank branch used to employ twenty workers. The spread of ATMs reduced that number to about thirteen, making it cheaper for banks to open branches. Meanwhile, the number of banking transactions soared, and banks began to compete by promising better customer service: more bank employees, at more branches, handling more complex tasks than tellers in the past. More recently, personal devices and cloud-based financial transactions are further changing the work of banks. While more than 8,000 US bank branches have closed over a decade (an average of more than 150 per state) and more than 90 percent of transactions now take place online, the number of US bank employees remained relatively stable at more than two million.[12] Bank branches remain a brick-and-mortar presence, but the tellers may help customers with a smartphone or tablet in hand. Or customers may find a teller online now; it's a role exemplified in Bank of America's new experiment with hybrid banking, small unstaffed mini-branches that offer a direct link to tellers via video conference.[13]

The ATM story is an important parable for business leaders, workers, and policymakers. It vividly shows why simplistic ideas like "technology replaces human jobs" are simultaneously so enticing and misleading. Solving the organizational, social, and strategic challenges of work automation demands a pivotal future capability—optimizing the constantly evolving options that combine human and automated work.

Some bank teller tasks are indeed highly susceptible to automation that replaces the human worker, such as "documenting/recording information" and "interacting with computers." Others are unlikely to be substituted by automation but might be augmented by improved information or algorithmic decision rules, such as "assisting and caring for others," "resolving conflicts and negotiating with others," and "interpreting the meaning of information for others." Still other tasks will likely be reinvented by the combination of humans and automation, such as "making decisions and solving problems," where the automated databases and decision rules would improve the knowledge and judgment of humans in ways not possible without automation. The end result is an evolving bank teller job that today contains few of the traditional repetitive tasks but now includes remote human tellers whose work is systematically enhanced by a collaboration with automation.

Even today, organization leaders are often presented with automation proposals based on a logic of "replacing jobholders with automation," which calculate the returns to automation in terms of reduced employment costs. To be sure, cost efficiency is seldom the only goal, with many organizations investing in automation to improve speed, reliability, insight, and customer value. Yet, even with these goals, the operating model is frequently to shift human work to automation, with little thought nor useful frameworks to tackle the questions of how to combine human workers with automation. Automation efforts frequently crash on the rocks of poorly thought out work design and redesign. A new work operating system that deconstructs and reinvents human work into tasks and capabilities offers the solution to this dilemma.

Boundaryless Ecosystem of Work Arrangements

Increasingly, work is done by workers who are not regular full-time employees. The new work operating system considers the work independently of any particular arrangement. Engaging such workers requires incorporating work arrangements that go beyond the typical assumption that the worker will be an employee who holds a series of jobs within the organization. Examples of these new work arrangements include the following:

- contractors
- freelancers
- volunteers
- gig workers
- internal talent marketplaces—full-time employees working on projects and assignments across the organization and beyond their job

To be sure, regular full-time employment in jobs should also be on this list, but it should not be the only option. Rather, it should be one of several options that are optimized to best engage workers. However, for most organizations, the list includes only employees in jobs. Even if the options include contractors, the management of the contractor workforce is often separated and assigned to the procurement function, with HR and procurement discouraged or even prohibited from sharing their systems, let alone optimizing combinations of contractors and employees.

Workers as a "Whole Person" with Deconstructed Capabilities (e.g., Skills)

How should organizations and society account for the capabilities of individuals, workers, and potential workers? Traditionally, organizations have attached worker capability to their job, with most HR systems focusing on whether or not a person is qualified for an entry-level job or is qualified to move to a new job within the organization. Training programs are designed to prepare workers for one or another job, and traditional work systems track what jobs individuals have held. The traditional resume lists previous job titles and duties. Traditionally, educational institutions have accounted for learning by conferring degrees, comprised as lists of successfully completed courses that were part of a particular "major." Putting the two together, the traditional work operating system constructs intact jobs with a set of qualifications and then searches for candidates who possess the proper intact degrees that include a set of classes, rejecting those who are not "fully qualified."

Seeing work and workers in this way is a recipe for suboptimization. First, when a worker's qualifications are embedded in a school degree, or in the job titles they have held, their capabilities unrelated to the degree or the job become invisible. A common example happens in retail organizations that are automating elements of the customer experience, such as store checkout. If you only know that the workers have held the job of "cashier," it's tempting to think that your organization must lay off all the cashiers and hire new workers to maintain and program the automated checkout system. The traditional work system tells nothing about the workers beyond their qualifications to be cashiers.

Yet, it is common that the workers holding the cashier jobs may have completed online or community college courses that provide qualifications for tasks such as computer coding and systems analysis. The workers often have adjacent capabilities that partially qualify them for the new work. A traditional work system based on jobs and jobholders will miss the possibility that the cashiers could become systems analysts or coders because that work operating system cannot see the adjacent skills held by the "cashiers." This is often called "seeing the whole person" in organizations that adopt systems to map the full array of worker qualifications. Only some of those qualifications will be used in any job, but any one of which might become relevant as the work changes.

Second, the traditional work operating system, based on work as a job and worker as a jobholder, offers little opportunity to look beyond whether a worker is fully qualified for a job. If a worker hasn't held a job like the one being filled, then they can easily be categorized among the "unqualified." Yet, optimizing work increasingly requires a more nuanced approach. Particularly in times of labor shortages or rapid change, the right question is not "is a worker fully qualified for this job" but rather "which potential workers are "mostly qualified", and what would it take to make them fully qualified?" Identifying the mostly qualified requires a work system capable of seeing workers as an array of capabilities rather than as a holder of a "degree" or a job. Identifying what it would take to bring the mostly qualified up to fully qualified similarly requires a system that can see the worker's array of capabilities and identify how adding a few particular new capabilities would produce full qualifications.

Of course, actual systems are already a bit more nuanced. Most organizations track not only the jobs workers have held but also some system of more granular work capabilities, often called skills or competencies. Educational institutions are increasingly called upon to deconstruct their educational offerings, allowing students to drop in and out of the institution between employment periods and offering "stackable credentials"[14] that can add up to a degree over time but do not require a continuous stint at the college to achieve the degree. We see the start of systems that deconstruct individual capabilities in the same way that jobs are deconstructed into task elements.

The New Work Operating System Principles

The four principles of the new work operating system are the following:

1. Start with the work (current and future tasks) and not the existing jobs.
2. Combine humans and automation.
3. Consider the full array of human work engagements (e.g., employment, gig, freelance, alliances, projects, other alternative work arrangements).
4. Allow talent to "flow" to work versus being limited to fixed, traditional jobs.

Each of these principles offers a useful contrast between the new and the traditional work operating system. Next, we'll describe each principle in turn.

Start with the Work, Not the Current or Future Jobs

The traditional work operating system starts with jobs and employees within the organization, creating several major challenges. Consider the challenge of implementing new process automation. The typical operating system must frame the work design through questions like "What jobs will be eliminated due to automation?" and "What training will keep my existing employees relevant?" and "What do I need to pay to get the needed skilled employees?"

These questions take a myopic view of work and therefore overlook important opportunities and challenges. The new work operating system starts with different questions:

- "What are the current and future work tasks (regardless of current jobs)?"
- "What are the capabilities to perform these tasks?"
- "What current and potential workers have or might develop those capabilities (regardless of their current job)?"
- "What are the best work arrangements to engage those capabilities (including options beyond regular full-time employment)?"

Combine Humans and Automation

The traditional work operating system assumes automation substitutes for human workers. The actual relationship is far more nuanced, and this is captured by the new work operating system. Depending on the characteristics of the tasks and objectives, automation can either substitute, augment, or transform human work. The new work operating system offers better questions for organizations to ask the following:

- What are the elemental tasks within the process?
- What are the characteristics of each task (repetitive versus variable, mental versus physical, independent versus interactive)?

- What is the objective we are trying to solve for each task?
- Does automation substitute for the human, augment the human, or create new work?
- What are the available types of automation (robotic process automation, cognitive automation, or social or collaborative robotics)?
- What is the optimal way to combine human and automated work across jobs and processes?

Notice how the first question immediately reframes the analysis to focus on the deconstructed tasks rather than on the entire job. With that fundamental reframing, the rest of the analysis is more optimal.

We have noted the recent significant increase in work automation in a variety of domains, often accelerated by the COVID-19 pandemic. Robots in hospitals can now remotely monitor patients and take their temperatures, and robots in buildings can remotely clean and fog surfaces. We have also observed the growing interest and experiments with "dark" warehouses and manufacturing operations as a way to reduce the risk and danger to human workers as well as to reduce the risk of downtime when humans become ill. However, such innovations seldom remove all human work. Rather, the role of human talent evolves toward primarily solving problems and maintaining an almost completely automated facility, something we will explore later in the book. In all such cases, the work outcomes should be the result of a thoughtful application of a process like the one we just described versus merely looking to substitute a person in a job for a machine.

Let's take the example of robots in hospitals to illustrate the value of the questions above:

1. What are the elemental tasks within the process?

Rather than ask "will robots replace nurses?" we deconstruct the nursing job and notice that some nursing time is spent checking patients and doing very routine things like taking temperatures, while other time is spent on tasks that more fully use nursing credentials, such as attending to patient crises and administering medicine.

2. What are the characteristics of each task (repetitive versus variable, mental versus physical, independent versus interactive)?

Now we can see that the tasks of checking to see if a patient responds to a greeting and taking their temperature are repetitive, physical, and only slightly interactive, making these tasks ripe for automation. On the other hand, tasks such as attending to patient crises and administering medicine are more variable, mental, and interactive, making them appropriate for human nurses and more fitting with nurse qualifications.

3. What is the objective we are trying to solve for each task?

Tasks such as taking a temperature and getting a response to a greeting add value mostly by being done to a minimum standard and avoiding obvious mistakes. On the other hand, tasks such as attending to patient crises and administering medicine must meet a very high standard, where the quality of performance makes a very large difference to the outcome. Of course, having nurses take patients' temperatures might help a patient's recovery through the positive effects of human social interactions. This is a good example of how job deconstruction clarifies how the work serves the objective. Separating the tasks of "human interaction" from "taking temperatures" allows us to see that if nurses are routinely administering medications to patients, the human interaction will still take place.

4. Does automation substitute for the human, augment the human, or create new work?

Now that we have isolated the deconstructed tasks, we can see that the robots can indeed substitute for the human nurse in taking temperatures and checking on patients. In some ways, this automation has augmented the human nurse by freeing them up to focus on tasks where their capabilities are far more pivotal.

5. What are the available types of automation (robotic process automation, cognitive automation, or social or collaborative robotics)?

Automating the task of taking temperatures and checking on patients might be done with robotic process automation, where a patient monitor might feed the data directly into a database. The solution might also use cognitive automation (or AI) if the patient monitors are programmed to alert nurses when a patient demonstrates a pattern of unresponsiveness or has a series of consecutive high temperature readings. Finally, the solution might use "social" robotics, where robots physically move among patients and interact with the nurses.

6. What is the optimal way to combine human and automated work across jobs and processes?

By deconstructing the nurse's job, we can now see that it is a careful combination of a human nurse and a robotic assistant that optimizes the work process. This redefines the work beyond the nurse job description. It also means that nurses are now likely to collaborate closely with robotics designers, technicians, and maintenance persons.

Consider the Full Array of Human Work Engagements

Even when automation is not an issue, or in addition to work automation, the future of work will embody alternative work arrangements. That means work arrangements that are different from, and go beyond, regular full-time employment in jobs. Optimal solutions seldom directly substitute an alternative work arrangement for an entire job. Rather, the optimum solution is apparent only if we deconstruct the job and examine how each task is best accomplished.

Three fundamental dimensions and questions define and suggest how to optimize alternative work arrangements:[15]

1. The assignment (or the work to be done)
   a. How small can it be deconstructed?
   b. How widely can it be dispersed?
   c. How far from employment can it be detached?
2. The organization (the boundary containing the work)
   a. How easily can the organization boundary be permeated?
   b. How strongly should the organization link with others?

   c. How deeply should the task involve collaboration?

   d. How extensively should the boundary be flexed to include others?

3. The rewards (the elements of exchange for the work)

   a. How small or immediate the time frame?

   b. How specifically to individualize?

   c. How creatively to imagine beyond traditional pay and benefits?

For example, organizations contain the job of product designer, which includes many tasks. One of those tasks is generating ideas for new products or features, combined with other tasks such as evaluating those ideas to fit with existing production or marketing strategies and selling the ideas to key organization constituents. If we deconstruct the job, then the task of generating new product ideas emerges as one "assignment" that can be deconstructed from the rest of the job. That task can be undertaken by volunteer focus groups, perhaps comprised of regular customers, dispersed to a wide array of volunteers and detached from an employment contract. The "organization" boundary must be permeated but only enough to allow the volunteers to interact with product design teams. The "rewards" consist of free products or even just the fun of participating and can be offered on an immediate time frame.

Notice, however, that if the question is framed as "can volunteer focus groups do the job of product designer?" the answer is simply "no," and this alternative does not present itself. Similarly, if the question is framed as "how can we design a job that consists only of suggesting new products and features?" the answer is "impossible" because the organization does not have enough of such work to fill a regular job.

Once work is deconstructed, the individual tasks present a much wider range of human work options. The options might include employees in full- or part-time jobs at your location, employees in full- or part-time jobs at other locations, employees in other parts of your organization who you could tap for a project or assignment, independent contractors (either engaged directly or through gig platforms like Upwork and Toptal), the talent of an outsourcer, or the talent of an alliance partner.

Allow Talent to Flow to Work versus Being Dedicated to Fixed, Permanent Jobs

Talent should flow to work. Sometimes that can involve regular full-time employees in jobs, but even those jobs should be considered fungible. Flowing often requires that workers look beyond their strict job descriptions to apply their capabilities where they are most pivotal, such as when business analysts, data scientists, and software developers flow to a project to develop new functionality for a customer-facing application.

The key is to optimally and perpetually reinvent work by combining options such as the following:

1. Talent in fixed roles with regular full-time employees, perhaps due to a convenient volume of work that fits a regular job or unique or difficult-to-acquire skills that justify offering a fixed full-time assignment

2. Talent who flows to tasks and assignments or projects, perhaps because their enabling capabilities are required in short-term specific bursts, by several different work processes (such as a freelancer or project-based data scientist who moves between projects in marketing, HR, and operations as needed)

3. Talent who are in hybrid roles that are partially fixed because of work volume or skills dedicated to a job but can also flow to specific challenges as needed (such roles often emerge from internal talent marketplaces where regular jobholders take on additional project work)

The guiding questions for determining how to optimize fixed, flow, and hybrid work arrangements are like those listed above that refer to alternative work arrangements. Now, the questions would be applied to workers who are employees, so the question of detaching tasks from employment doesn't apply. When it comes to "boundary" questions, the focus is now not on the organization boundary but on the boundary between different organization units or jobs within the organization boundary.

Deconstruction Is Vital to Organizational Agility

How do organizations, workers, and societies pivot from this legacy work operating system? The principle of agility both motivates this pivot and reveals how to implement it.

The notion of Agile processes is well established in the arena of software development. It is supplanting the legacy system of the "waterfall," which requires that each stage of software development be completed and then sent "down the waterfall" to the next stage, with little opportunity to move backward to earlier steps. The Agile approach, in contrast, approaches a project as a simultaneous collaboration between the different stages, with the software being continually tested against user behaviors and requirements and updated versions rolled out on an ongoing basis.

Many organizations have adopted the Agile approach to transform their mindset and work processes beyond software development, guided by Agile's three relevant core values:

1. Prioritize individuals and interactions over processes and tools.
2. Prioritize customer collaboration over contract negotiation.
3. Prioritize responding to change over following a plan.

Those values are particularly vital to pivot to the new work operating system, yet the Agile process redesign alone cannot overcome the constraints imposed by traditional ways of thinking about jobs. A major consumer goods organization implemented Agile, but despite its thoughtful approach to redesigning its processes, and even upskilling its employees, the company faced major difficulty in getting its employees to flow to work and actively engage with challenges that spanned job titles or departments. For example, customer complaints received by call center employees revealed needed product improvements that had to be implemented by product designers/developers. The Agile process design revealed an obvious solution: the call center representatives and the designers/developers would flow to this challenge, working together. However, in reality the call center representatives who received customer complaints did not see it as their job to convey them to product designers and developers. Similarly, the product designers/developers did not see it as their job to ask or even listen to the call center employees' experience with customer complaints. The legacy work system relied on job descriptions to represent the work and jobholders to represent the workers' capabilities. Thus, much of the pivotal value of the Agile process design was squandered because the workers were trapped in a system of jobs that offered no mechanism to flow to the goal of product improvement.

The organization lacked the capacity to deconstruct the jobs into discrete tasks that clearly supported its goals, so its workers struggled with work that reached beyond their jobs. They were challenged to understand how projects fit with their day jobs, how to find space to contribute, and how to respond to direct supervisors who felt that projects were unrelated to the employees' functional areas.

The History of Work Deconstruction

Work will be better optimized if work systems break free of a legacy system defined by jobs and jobholders. This idea builds upon decades of research that recognizes the importance of the foundational deconstructed elements of jobs and jobholders. This prior work has not yet yielded a new work operating system that we describe in this book, but it provides important context. First, it is useful to recognize the contributions of this prior work. Second, it is instructive to understand how even this important and useful prior work did not yield the new work operating system that we describe due to a continuing fixation on connecting the work with that legacy system of jobs and jobholders.

Taylorism (circa 1920)

One can say that methods for work deconstruction date back as early as the dawn of the industrial revolution. The title of our book *Work without Jobs* might reasonably conjure up images of relentless atomization and commoditization of work as well as images of a workplace with nothing but deconstructed work elements, leaving workers and leaders to try to navigate their way toward productive and systematic progress without any guidance at all. Neither is fully correct, but both are indeed relevant to explaining our approach and its value.

Students of the history of work will vividly recall that Frederick W. Taylor, in the 1920s, was one of the first proponents of work deconstruction and reconstruction. The most widely shared impression of "Taylorism" is that it was an attempt to exploit workers by ruthlessly identifying the most productive way to do every task and then reconstructing the work to rigidly require that every worker adhere to the single best method. In principle, this sort of task-based "scientific management" would produce more optimal work methods, less worker injury and fatigue, and higher and fairer pay levels because all workers would learn and conduct their work in the most optimal way, through a set of well-studied task behaviors.

As Richard Salame noted in 2018,

> It's hard to overstate how far efficiency engineers went to measure and surveil workers' bodies. They used stopwatches, photographed and filmed workers, and tied lightbulbs to workers' fingers to trace hand movements across long-exposure photographs. One engineer, Frank Gilbreth, disaggregated each finger, shoulder, and foot, plotting individual movements in units of a thousandth of a minute. Workers were made to study the evidence of their own inadequacies and learn better methods. Those who could not meet the new standards were fired. . . . Decades before the video camera appeared in workplaces—let alone software to monitor computer-based work—this proselyting network of consultants and engineers brought together mechanical surveillance, iterative performance review, management by data, and individual monitoring in experiments and widely distributed tracts.[16]

Salame noted the similarities—and dangers—of such approaches in dehumanizing and commoditizing work: "The latest scandal to emerge from Amazon's warehouses centers on the company's newly patented wristband, which gives it the ability to track and record employees' hands in real time. Some have described the technology as a 'dystopian' form of surveillance. Amazon has countered that journalists are engaging in 'misguided' speculation. To hear the retail giant tell it, all

the device does is move its inventory-tracking equipment from workers' hands to their wrists—what's the big deal?"[17]

The End of the Job (circa 1994)

One popular past depiction of work without jobs is a 1994 *Fortune* article,
"The End of the Job," in which William Bridges described a fundamental
premise of this book: work organized into jobs was an artifact of the industrial revolution, and future societies would look back and note that many
of the frictions and dilemmas of the 1990s resulted from a futile attempt to
conceive and manage work within the confines of jobs in organizations.

Bridges suggested that "the single organization pattern that is free
from this built-in bias is the project cluster." He wrote, "Today's organization is rapidly being transformed from a structure built out of jobs
into a field of work needing to be done. Jobs are artificial units super-
imposed on this field. They are patches of responsibility that, together,
are supposed to cover the work that needs to be done. His job is to take
care of this, hers is to take care of that, and yours is to take care of the
other thing. Together you usually get the work done, though there are
always scraps and pieces of work that don't quite fall into anyone's job
description, and over time job responsibilities have to be adjusted and
new jobs added to keep getting everything done."[18]

Bridges described Intel, where new hires are assigned to a project that
changes over time and the person's responsibilities and tasks change
with it. The person is then assigned to another project (well before
the first project is finished) and so on. These projects require working
under several team leaders, keeping different schedules, being in various places, and performing several different tasks. Bridges noted that
"hierarchy implodes, not because someone theorizes that it should but
because under these conditions it cannot be maintained."[19]

Bridges's article, with its example of Intel as a project-based and self-
organized work system, is compelling. Yet even today, the vast majority
of all work systems still use the job and the jobholder as the fundamental
unit for managing work. The promise of a new work model suggested by
Bridges still awaits such a work system freed from static jobs.

Work Crafting . . . The Worker as the Work Designer

Amy Wrzeniewski and Jane Dutton coined the term *job crafting* in 2001, noting that even with fixed jobs, workers may have some discretion in their work tasks, relationships, and the meaning they attach to their work tasks.[20] Evidence suggests this can have positive effects. Arnold Bakker and Evangelia Demorouti noted that through job crafting, workers can reduce work strain, increase work challenges, and thus increase their work engagement.[21] Alessandra Lazazzara, Maria Tims, and Davide de Gennaro reviewed the existing studies, offering a framework where workers may be proactive (to reach desirable goals or improve performance) or reactive (coping with organizational change and pressure) and can involve either "approach" (improving work and interpreting work stressors positively) or "avoidance" (reduce or eliminate negative job elements).[22] Even though these approaches are typically called job crafting, they rely on deconstructed job elements to understand and define both the work content that jobholders change and the process through which they change it. They noted that job crafting can result in both positive (meaningfulness, recognition, job satisfaction) and negative (regrets, overload, stress, health problems) outcomes.

Holacracy

There have been recent experiments and speculations about organizations designed completely as "swarms" of workers, finding their way to projects or tasks that are constantly in flux. Workers might flow toward the work tasks or projects with the greatest value, and a shared sense of purpose and strategic direction would guide them to combine those tasks and projects into the best work for each worker, and the best work arrangement (freelance, contract, employment, etc.), with far less friction from traditional things like jobs, functions, hierarchies, and managers.

A good example of this emerged under the term "holacracy," with perhaps the most popular rendition being associated with Zappos, and widely touted by its founder, Tony Hseih, circa 2015 and 2016. The system was based upon a self-managed work system created by Brian Robertson and his company HolacracyOne. The system replaces a hierarchy

with "super-circles" that reflect broad functions like marketing, "subcir-
cles" that reflect subprocesses like "digital advertising," and then roles
such as "social media producer" and "tasks" within those roles.[23] The
circles contain people in the role of "lead links" who assign work and
ensure it is completed. What's different is that as long as the circle work
is completed, the circle members can shift to pursue other projects, so
how the work is completed is determined on the fly. Thus, with its fundamental basis in roles and tasks, holacracy also reflects the notion of
work deconstruction, and in its encouragement of fluid work organization, the holacracy concept reflects the idea of perpetual work reconstruction and reinvention.

However, our new work operating model does not advocate nor
require that organizations fully abandon things like jobs and hierarchies.
Evidence suggests the optimum level of deconstruction-reconstruction
depends on the situation and that traditional jobs and hierarchies may
offer the right solution in many contexts. *The Atlantic* noted that such
flattened and less hierarchical work arrangements do not always prove
preferable to managers and workers.[24] One Stanford study found that egal-
itarian work structures were disorienting.[25] Workers found hierarchical
companies were more predictable, and therefore preferable, because it
was easy to figure out who did what and how compensation should be
doled out. Jeffrey Pfeffer of Stanford looked at why hierarchical structures in the workplace have such staying power and concluded perhaps
the obvious: they are practical and psychologically comforting.[26]

The New Work Operating System Is Foundational to Innovative Organization Designs

Taylorism, the end of the job, job crafting, holacracy, and a host of
other management ideas reveal the inherent requirement for a new
work operating system that allows for—but does not require—work
arrangements that include jobs and hierarchies or delves deeply into
worker actions and behaviors to identify best practices. We propose
that work deconstruction and reconstruction is a vital foundational

element for management and organizational design systems that range from Taylorism to holacracy, whether the result is a completely fluid organization structure like holacracy or a more fluid version of the traditional system of jobs and jobholders. What has been missing is the playbook that helps leaders, workers, policymakers, and organizational designers to understand how to accomplish that fluid deconstruction and reconstruction process, particularly within the framework of organizational agility.

Our point is that without this new work operating system, even the debate about these important issues is hamstrung within an often-obsolete concept that work must occur within jobs and workers must be jobholders. This limitation hinders work and organizational invention, social policy alternatives, public debate, relationships between worker collectives and organizations, and so on. Thus, our goal is not to endorse nor replicate any specific management proposal or system but to provide a playbook for work reconstruction that will enhance its practical application and thus accelerate these debates based on a more useful fundamental operating system.

This book describes how work deconstruction and reconstruction offer a new work operating system. Inevitably, workers themselves will deconstruct and reconstruct work as they gain greater insight into the new work operating system and the reinvention process it supports. This means that workers likely influence and even explicitly shape their own work deconstruction and reinvention. Both workers and the organizations that employ them will be important parties to job deconstruction and reinvention, so both workers and leaders will experience engagement with the process itself.

Seven Elements Distinguish the New from the Traditional Work Operating System

The new work operating system contrasts sharply with the traditional work operating system, as summarized in the following table, and is illustrated in the next chapters.

The new work operating system	The traditional work operating system
Work as deconstructed job elements (tasks)	Work as intact and mostly stable jobs
Work automation as optimizing task-level combinations of human and automated work	Work automation as replacing employees in jobs
Work arrangements including a boundaryless and democratized work ecosystem	Full-time employees inside a fixed organization boundary
Workers as a whole person with an array of deconstructed capabilities (e.g., skills)	Workers as jobholders with capability to fill "job requirements"
Perpetually reinvented task/project combinations and work arrangements beyond traditional employment	Stable system of jobs and employment contracts
Management and work coordination as collaborative hubs of teams and projects, aligned goals/purpose, and integrated through human/AI platforms and HR systems	Management and work coordination through hierarchy, structure, and stable reporting relationships
Social values and policies that enable and rely on fluid work arrangements and holistic worker capability to achieve worker sustainability, voice, equity, and inclusion	Social values and policies that rely on traditional jobs and employment to achieve worker sustainability, voice, equity, and inclusion

1 Work as Deconstructed Job Elements versus Stable Jobs

While legacy systems might once have been a pillar of competitive advantage, they are increasingly an obstacle to agility, particularly when it comes to the future of work.[1] There are few more visible or strong markers of legacy systems than the idea that work is contained in intact and stable jobs. Dating back to the beginning of the second industrial revolution, this concept has shaped how work is done and organized within organizations, how workers are rewarded, how education is designed, and how much of socioeconomic policy is structured.

So, how can you start the journey of creating a more agile, flexible, inclusive, and resilient enterprise that is built upon a new work system, a work system with the capacity to perpetually deconstruct work, deploy work tasks and activities to the most optimal work arrangement (employees, AI, robotics, gig talent, alliance partners, outsourcers, etc.), and reconstruct new, fundamentally different jobs and arrangements all while seamlessly integrating the various work options? As with most significant changes, a good start is to identify an opportunity to serve as a proof of concept and use that experience to motivate and guide broader adoption. A good proof of concept opportunity will illuminate the how the new work operating system presents success opportunities and what it requires.

Thus, you need not start by applying the new work operating system to your entire domain of work. Our experience suggests that there are already likely to be several high-value opportunities or trigger points where you can start:

1. Operating challenges: These are situations where you are rethinking workflows or processes such as manufacturing, information systems, customer service, and supply chains. For example, a new and unforeseen variable (e.g., political conflict, war, or disease outbreak) might remove a traditional supply chain source. COVID-19 forced companies to rapidly relocate previously offshored work to closer locations or to pivot from one manufacturing focus (making automobiles) to another (making ventilators). The capability to deconstruct and redeploy work was pivotal to resilience in the face of such unforeseen challenges.[2]

2. Constraints: These are bottlenecks in the things like talent pipelines, supply chains, information flows, or financial systems. They manifest as increasing costs or shortages in a workflow or an inability to find sufficient resources such as talent. For example, prior to the COVID-19 pandemic, many companies sought to attract individuals from a limited pool of digital talent (data scientists, application developers, AI programmers). By deconstructing work, some of the tasks in these jobs can be met through automation or alternative work arrangements.

3. Introduction of new technology: These situations occur when technological advances such as AI and robotics demand changes in processes and work that are too rapid for traditional systems. Most organizations tend to lead with the technology, not the work. A common presumption is that technology implementation will simply substitute for workers in jobs, delivering return on investment through labor cost reductions. Or it is assumed that the work will simply adjust to the new technology. This can lead to breakdowns in processes because of insufficient consideration of the human factor. By deconstructing work and workers, such problems can be more easily avoided by reinventing work at the task and capability level.

4. Shifts in organizational priorities: It is increasingly the case that organizations strive to achieve priorities beyond shareholder value, such as purpose, social contribution, inclusiveness, community contribution, equity, and environmental protection. Such shifts or additions to priorities often involve rethinking the way work contributes or the

role of workers. By deconstructing work, options emerge that are not apparent in the traditional job-based system, such as achieving some objectives through projects or inside gigs.

Once you have identified a trigger point where there is an opportunity to implement a proof of concept of the new work operating system, it is time to turn to the actual process for deconstructing jobs and jobholders. The characteristics of individual tasks are essential to identifying how they can be reconstructed into new jobs as well as what alternative work arrangements and work automation options are best.

Guiding Questions for Deconstructing Jobs

Job deconstruction starts by isolating the relevant work elements (such as tasks, activities, or projects) and what new elements are also relevant. Here, "relevant" means necessary or pivotal to achieving a process outcome, constituent need, or organizational strategic goal:

- What current activities/tasks are still relevant?
- What current activities/tasks are no longer relevant?
- What new relevant activities/tasks must be included?
- What is the timing or sequence of the relevant tasks?
- Where/how/when/what tasks should be performed and by whom?

The next step is to understand how improved performance actually creates value. This is the "return on improved performance," or ROIP.[3] ROIP can take many forms, but we can illustrate the power of the idea with four prototypical ROIP relationships. We will use tax preparation as our main example.

Reduce mistakes. This type of ROIP is most applicable when performance differences range from very low to the minimally acceptable level. For tax form preparation, this would span performance at a very low level with many mistakes or missing deadlines up to minimally acceptable performance that generates a small positive value. For tax preparation, ROIP by reducing mistakes would entail completing forms correctly and on time.

Reduce variance. This type of ROIP applies when performance differences have no impact on value, as when there are many ways to reach the same goal. Reducing variance produces value not in improving the outcome but in reaching that outcome in a more uniform way, often reducing costs or confusion. For tax preparation, this would include completing the tax form at any time before the due date since getting the tax form completed earlier adds no more value than completing the form on time, or when workers assemble components in different sequences but the final assembly is essentially identical.

Incrementally improve value. This type of ROIP is used when performance improvement produces a constant incremental increase in value. In tax form preparation, this ROIP range might reflect the clarity and grammar quality of the summary letter that accompanies a client's tax form. A minimally clear letter satisfies the minimum requirement, but if the letter is more clearly written and/or points out more important highlights, then that is incrementally more valuable to the client and the organization. Another example is when a call center representative upsells customers in incremental ways by suggesting additional features or faster shipping.

Exponentially improve value. This type of ROIP occurs when improved performance increases value exponentially. This range often represents very rare or creative performance that surprises and delights a customer or disruptively improves a process. In tax form preparation, this ROIP might reflect discovering an obscure tax deduction or a very sophisticated way to restate income to significantly reduce taxes owed Or, it might involve an in-store retail associate or call center representative uncovering obscure customer information that reveals a customer's unusual need for higher-margin products or services.

These are the guiding questions for ROIP for each work element:

- Will improved performance reduce mistakes?
- Will improved performance reduce variance?
- Will improved performance incrementally improve value?
- Will improved performance exponentially improve value?

Understanding each task is the foundation of work deconstruction.

Illustrating Job Deconstruction in a Retail Distribution Center

Our work with the distribution center of a major retailer will become our running case study to illustrate the four principles and other elements of the new work operating system in action. In brief, this retailer introduced new technology to automate the process of sorting products destined for retail stores and then packing those sorted products into small totes. These prepacked totes would significantly reduce the time that store employees spent restocking shelves.

Surprisingly, this new technology actually increased the number of jobs in the distribution center. This happened because the newly automated processes required new jobs to respond to the additional work created by the machine and the unforeseen complexities it introduced. For example, the company created a new role to provide the maintenance necessary on the new and more technically intricate equipment and a "problem solver" job to remove items that would get stuck in the machine or totes packed too full for the new machines to close. The results were suboptimal, including both higher than expected labor costs and below expected machine performance. As we will see in chapter 2, this was because the new automation had been retrofitted into a traditional existing work operating system, one that confined work only to employees in regular full-time jobs with fixed boundaries.

The retailer implemented a different solution based on our new work operating system. The design team first deconstructed the existing jobs, revealing the full array of tasks associated with the automation-enhanced process. The analysis examined the human worker tasks prior to automation and identified which tasks would automation replace humans, which tasks would automation augment human work, and what new tasks would be required in the automated process. This task-level analysis freed leaders to think outside the box of jobs and jobholders. For example, instead of creating a new job of problem solver, the new work operating system revealed that the task of blockage removal could be distributed to a worker in an existing packer job.

Instead of simply asking whether prior jobs should be retained or removed, the analysis revealed that certain jobs should be combined or reconfigured with parts of several previous jobs. For example, the company determined the number of activities from the picker role such as moving empty and filled totes that could be moved to the packer job since that job required similar skills to those possessed by current packers.

Let's illustrate how the organization applied deconstruction as it adopted the new work operating system. Our example will focus on the packing subset of the overall process. The deconstructed activities are described below. For each task, we have also described the ROIP, which refers to the value created through higher performance.

1. *Pick up and assemble totes:* The ROIP is to incrementally improve performance for faster throughput.

2. *Move each tote to a packing location:* The ROIP is to reduce variation, doing the task the same way every time.

3. *Pull the labeled product from the bulk container:* The ROIP is to reduce variation, doing the task the same way every time.

4. *Scan the product label:* The ROIP is to eliminate mistakes, ensuring that every product label is scanned.

5. *Insert/pack pulled product in appropriate tote:* The ROIP is to reduce variation, doing the task the same way every time.

6. *Adjust/repack product in totes:* The ROIP is to incrementally improve the packing to optimize space while maintaining the integrity of the product.

7. *Pull the packed tote, scan, and move to shipping location:* This task involves seeing when a tote is full, pulling it out, closing it up, and moving it to an appropriate shipping location. The ROIP is to incrementally improve the integrity of the closed tote and placement in the right location.

Let's explore each of the activities in this subset of the overall process in some detail.

The first activity in this "pack" portion of the workflow is the work of picking and assembling the totes that would be used to ship product from the distribution center to the retail store. The performance value in these tasks is incrementally improving their speed and accuracy. The next task in the process involves associating the assembled tote with a pack location followed by the task of pulling labeled products from the bulk containers and then scanning the label on the product to determine which tote it should be assigned to. The performance value in these tasks is reducing variance. Immediately after this, the pulled product is inserted/packed in the appropriate tote. This work too has a performance value of reducing variance, like the previous tasks. The next work element is adjusting/repacking the products in the tote in a way that ensures there is sufficient space for additional products but still protects the product from potential damage. The performance value of this work element is incrementally improving the packing speed and the efficiency of the packing pattern. The packed tote is then pulled aside, scanned, and moved to the shipping location. The performance value of this final task is to improve speed and accuracy.

Deconstructing the work from jobs to tasks is essential, and at first it can be unfamiliar and time consuming. However, there is a growing array of tools to expedite and streamline this analysis. Such tools typically employ existing databases of work elements such as O*Net or ESCO. The tools use AI and user input to match the tasks from the actual deconstructed jobs to the tasks in the databases. This allows the tasks being analyzed to be rated on the dimensions that are included in the database, such as automation potential and skill level.

The Genentech case described next shows a practical example work deconstruction in action.

Work Deconstruction at Genentech

Genentech is a leading biotechnology company and a member of the Roche Group. Like many other organizations, Genentech had long sought to increase the flexibility with which its talent engaged with work so as to increase their engagement and retention while making the company attractive to new hires. However, its efforts were often stymied by the various aspects of the traditional work operating system that we described in the introduction, particularly the notion of functionally oriented jobs as being the primary means for work. Previous efforts to introduce flexible ways of working often ran into concerns that some jobs could not be performed at alternative locations, times, or means. The COVID-19 pandemic accelerated the organization's desire to reframe flexibility and update its philosophy to overcome the legacy framing of jobs and create equitable access to various flexible work options.

Led by Chief People and Culture Officer Cynthia Burks and Global Head of Portfolio and Product Development Strategy Rhona O'Leary, the organization embarked on an agile transformation journey to develop a future of working strategy that would be both inclusive of all talent and aligned to the various types of work across the organization. An agile sprint team made up of employees from across the organization met on a biweekly basis to document the current state, analyze the work, develop, test recommendations, and plan for the change. The team began by developing a set of guiding principles that would guide their work and the strategy's development. The principles covered a variety of areas including the impact on business performance, employee engagement, company culture, and commitment to sustainability. The team then engaged employees and leaders at each stage of the journey, from seeking their input at the beginning on the key pain opportunity areas to engaging them in testing the overall architecture of the future of working strategy to brainstorming on the best ways to implement it and drive change. The voices of those closest to the work were pivotal to ensuring that the solution worked and every stakeholder was part of the journey.

Deconstruction was essential to getting the future of working strategy right. It allowed the team to move beyond jobs to the type of work being performed. The team decided to deconstruct a representative sample of jobs and identify the optimal location, times, and means for the component tasks for each job with the goal of providing more flexible work options to more of the workforce. Figure 1.1 illustrates the critical step of deconstructing the jobs and categorizing the component tasks along three continuums. The "when" continuum analyzed the time sensitivity of the task, the "where" continuum looked at whether the task was

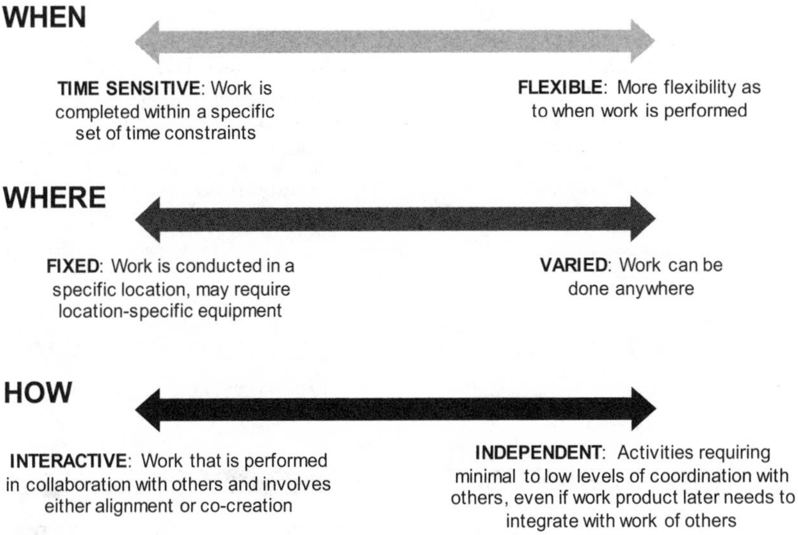

WHEN

TIME SENSITIVE: Work is
completed within a specific
set of time constraints

FLEXIBLE: More flexibility as
to when work is performed

WHERE

FIXED: Work is conducted in a
specific location, may require
location-specific equipment

VARIED: Work can be
done anywhere

HOW

INTERACTIVE: Work that is performed
in collaboration with others and involves
either alignment or co-creation

INDEPENDENT: Activities requiring
minimal to low levels of coordination with
others, even if work product later needs to
integrate with work of others

Figure 1.1
Genentech task/activity-level continuums

location dependent, and the "how" continuum looked at the degree of human interaction required to perform the task.

After the jobs were deconstructed into their component tasks and the tasks plotted on the continuums, the team created a set of personas based on where the activities fell on the various points of the continuum, as you will see below. The graphic below illustrates a subset of the personas developed by the team, where each persona is considered an archetype of many roles. For example, persona A involved work that was time sensitive, location specific, and performed independently. The roles that most represented this persona based on where most of their component tasks fell were the manufacturing technician, lab assistant, facilities engineer, IT infrastructure specialist, and building security.

While most employees should be able to "see" themselves in one of the personas based on the when/where/how factors that represent their work activity, it was recognized that there is often significant diversity in work activity within a single role and different individuals within the same role may find their work represented by different personas.

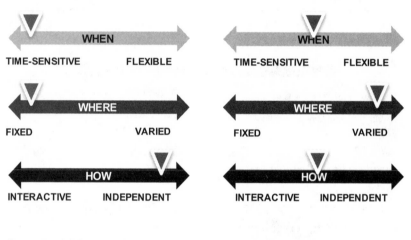

A: My work is independent and performed where my equipment or colleagues are located

Work is time-sensitive or needs to be performed at specified time
Work is conducted in a specific location and has a physical component
Work is done independently

B: My work is location-independent, with a mix of when and how I do it

Some work is time-constrained and some can be done at flexible times
Work can be conducted in a variety of places and is cognitive in nature
Some work is via co-creation, some asynchronous collaboration, some independent

WHEN
TIME-SENSITIVE   FLEXIBLE

WHERE
FIXED   VARIED

HOW
INTERACTIVE   INDEPENDENT

WHEN
TIME-SENSITIVE   FLEXIBLE

WHERE
FIXED   VARIED

HOW
INTERACTIVE   INDEPENDENT

Representative Roles:
Manufacturing Tech, **Lab Assistant**, Facilities Engineer, IT infrastructure specialist, Security

Representative Roles:
Development/Clinical Scientist, Project Team Leader and Project Manager, Molecule Development Team

Figure 1.2
Genentech example personas

For example, the job of a lab assistant might appear to have limited options for flexibility given the more visible aspects of the job like conducting experiments using specialist equipment. However, that role also includes tasks like reviewing research reports and analyzing data from experiments. These tasks do not have time constraints, can be performed anywhere, and are performed independently. As such, the role aligns to two different personas, as illustrated in figure 1.2.

The team then identified all the work options available within each of the three categories of when, where, and how and, based on the unique profile of activities for each persona, identified the options available to

C: My work is collaborative but not location- or time-specific

Work can be done at flexible times in a given day
Work can be conducted in a variety of places
Work is done collaboratively

D: My work does not have specific requirements of where, when, and how

Work is typically not time-constrained in a given day
Work can be conducted in a variety of places
Majority of work is done independently

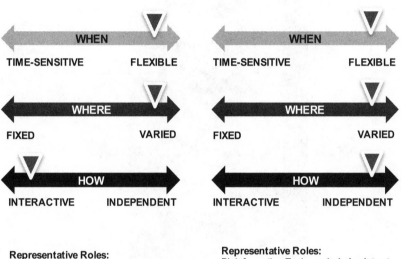

Representative Roles:
Benefits Manager,
Customer Engagement Team, HR Business Partners, Finance Business Partners

Representative Roles:
Bioinformatics Engineer, **Lab Assistant**
Patent Attorney

Figure 1.2
(continued)

each persona. Figure 1.3 illustrates a subset of the work options available to Genentech employees. As you will see, persona A is eligible for traditional on-campus work, scheduled remote work, a conventional forty-hour workweek, flexible start or stop times each day, regular full-time work, and job sharing (typically involving a couple of people sharing one job). This represented a significant departure from the legacy state whereby the roles that now aligned to persona A were often denied any flexibility on account of their need to be performed "in person and on site all the time."

Persona examples	WHERE			WHEN			HOW		
	On-campus	Scheduled remote	Remote work full-time	Conventional workweek	Flex start/ stop	Compressed workweek	Full-time	Part-time	Job sharing
A:	X	X		X	X		X		X
B:	X	X	X	X	X	X	X	X	X
C:	X	X	X	X	X	X	X	X	X
D:	X	X		X	X		X	X	X

Figure 1.3

Genentech work options by persona

Deconstruction was essential to enabling Genentech to create a more inclusive and equitable flexible work strategy. It enabled the organization to move beyond the typical blanket rules and beliefs about what flexibility should be available to various roles. The thoughtful approach employed by the Genentech team is helping the organization ensure the engagement of current talent and the attraction of new talent while preserving the collaboration and serendipitous connections that are so critical to its innovation-based strategy.

Recent research from the McKinsey Global Institute suggests that the disruptions caused by the COVID-19 pandemic in 2021 will likely result in organizations needing to create a more personalized and fluid work experience.[4] By analyzing the human interaction and the location of work (2 of the 3 continuums used by Genentech) for 800 occupations, the study determined that numerous trends that accelerated as a result of the pandemic like remote work, e-commerce, virtual transactions and automation/AI will either continue to accelerate or remain at levels materially above those of the pre-pandemic world.

Demonstrating Feasibility with a Proof of Concept

A proof of concept is a vital first step in adopting the new work operating system. As we demonstrated in the introduction, the new system is radically different from the traditional operating system, so getting started often requires demonstrating its value in a limited and targeted application. A proof of concept can enhance the chances of successfully implementing the new work operating system by

- creating the space and time to learn from and iterate on it before it is introduced more broadly,
- helping to identify the enablers and obstacles to its adoption (e.g., will the technology infrastructure support it, are the appropriate learning systems in place to upskill talent), and
- demonstrating the value of the new work operating system to leaders and stakeholders in other parts of the business.

Organizations need to approach implementing the new work operating system in the spirit of Agile experimentation, recognizing that
it will not be perfect in its first iteration. A proof of concept allows
Agile elements such as failing fast and rapidly iterating based on lessons learned along the way.

Conclusion

Deconstructing the jobs/jobholders and then reconstructing the work
more optimally takes effort, but by following the guidelines and questions we have provided here, jobs can be deconstructed and the work
can be more systematically and strategically focused. The effort pays
off in the form of better solutions and greater insight created using the
new work operating system.

The subsequent chapters will show how this first step of job deconstruction lays a foundation for a better approach to the other components
of the new work operating system, including automation, alternative
work arrangements, skills-based work, and leadership. We will explore
automation next in chapter 2 and will continue to use the retail company
case study to illustrate it. As we did in chapter 1, we will complement that
case with examples from other industries to illustrate the range of options
available when you contemplate work without jobs.

A Checklist for Getting Started

1. Have you identified a trigger point for a proof of concept opportunity?
2. Have you answered the key questions for deconstructing work?
3. Have you deconstructed tasks at a granular enough level such that
   you understand each task's ROIP?

2 Work Automation Deconstructed: Not Replacing Jobs with Automation but Optimizing Task-Level Combinations of Humans and Automation

The contrast between the traditional and the new work operating systems are perhaps most starkly apparent when we consider work automation, as in the ATM story in the introduction. Work automation is too often framed as "how many jobholders will new technology replace and at what labor cost savings?"

Should work automation replace people? This is a debate as old as the dawn of technology, famously illustrated by the Luddites,[1] who opposed automated textile manufacturing machines. The Luddites were a secret oath-based organization of English textile workers in the nineteenth century, a radical faction who protested by destroying textile machinery. The group is believed to have taken their name from Ned Ludd, a weaver. They protested manufacturers who used machines in what they called "a fraudulent and deceitful manner" to get around standard labor practices. Luddites feared that the time spent learning the skills of their craft would go to waste as machines would replace them.

As the COVID-19 crisis accelerated, work automation appeared to replace human jobholders. Scientists at the University of Liverpool had a new lab assistant with a very strong work ethic: a robot chemist that conducted experiments by itself.[2] The 1.75-meter-tall intelligent robot moved around the laboratory, avoiding human coworkers and obstacles while performing a wide range of different tasks independently. It could even decide for itself which tests to do next based on previous results. A cylindrical robot rolled into a treatment room to allow healthcare workers to remotely take temperatures and measure blood pressure and oxygen saturation from patients hooked up to a ventilator.[3] Another robot that looked like a pair of large fluorescent lights rotated vertically traveled throughout a hospital, disinfecting with ultraviolet light.[4] Meanwhile a cart-like robot brought food to people quarantined in a sixteen-story hotel.[5] Outside, quadcopter drones ferried test samples to laboratories[6] and watched for violations of stay-at-home restrictions.[7]

Did each of these work automation innovations replace some of the work of humans? Of course! It is true that costs may go down, risk may be reduced, and patients and customers may enjoy the novelty—in the short run. Are such solutions sustainable and correct for the longer run?

A closer look will reveal that what at first appear to be robots that replaced research scientists, nurses, cleaners, and enforcement officers are actually examples of new combinations of work automation with humans, in newly reconfigured task combinations. Focusing only on how automation replaces jobholders misses the most important point: automation seldom neatly replaces human jobholders with automation. Rather, the most innovative and optimal solutions are combinations of automation and human workers. However, perceiving, understanding, and optimizing those combinations requires liberating work from jobs and jobholders. The new work operating system, based on deconstruction, illuminates those more optimal combinations.

Chapter 1 showed how to deconstruct jobs into their elements, with a series of questions to guide that deconstruction. When work automation is an option, these additional characteristics of each task become relevant:

1. Is the task repetitive versus variable?
2. Is the task independent versus interactive?
3. Is the task physical versus mental?

The answers to these questions determine the automation potential of each task. There are many nuances, and each dimension is a continuum rather than simply an either-or. However, in general the tasks that are more repetitive, independent, and physical have greater automation potential.

This chapter will show how the new work operating system is vital to designing optimal combinations of humans and automation and explain how to use it to achieve those combinations. The characteristics of the deconstructed tasks or activities combine with the objective or ROIP from chapter 1 to determine where automation is optimal.

Recall from chapter 1 that the objective for each task reflects how improved performance creates value. There are four general categories:

- reduce mistakes
- reduce variance
- incrementally improve value
- exponentially improve value

With the automation potential and the ROIP determined, you are ready to consider the type of automation that might be best suited to the task. Automation falls in three broad types that will be defined below:

- robotic process automation (RPA)
- cognitive automation or AI
- social robotics

Finally, for each task, you can now consider the effect of automation, relative to the human worker. There are three possible effects:

- The human worker is substituted
- The human worker is augmented
- The human worker's value is reinvented

Three Types of Automation

RPA is the simplest and most mature of the three types of automation listed above. It automates high volume, low complexity, and routine tasks. For example, it has long been used to automate "swivel chair" tasks that used to require a person to "swivel" from one data source to another to transfer or connect data from disparate systems. A common application involves transferring data between software systems or using simple rules to find information in emails or spreadsheets and entering it into business systems like enterprise resource planning or customer relationship management (CRM). Process robotics can automate them quickly and cheaply, without requiring labor. RPA often *substitutes* for humans in highly repetitive, independent, mental work where the objective is to reduce variance.

Cognitive automation, often called AI, automates human cognition using tools like pattern recognition, machine learning, and language understanding. This "recognition intelligence" is a combination of AI, machine learning, and sensors. It is at the heart of automating tasks like voice and image recognition, voice conversion to text, and natural language understanding. Cognitive automation typically *augments* humans doing variable, independent, mental work with the objective of incrementally or exponentially improving value.

Social robotics refers to automated robots that interact with humans by moving among them, using sensors, AI, and machinery. A subset of social robotics is "collaborative" robotics (cobots). Cobots sense the human worker and adjust to the human behavior in real time, physically working with the human. Social robotics typically *augments* humans, doing variable, interactive, physical work with the objective of incrementally improving value.

Work Automation in the Retail Distribution Center

Returning to the retail distribution center, recall how the traditional work operating system led the retailer to view the work as binary combinations of humans in jobs to be replaced by the new technology. The traditional approach was to find the jobs where automation might replace humans. However, as the retailer analyzed the work, it found that automation replaced only some elements of existing jobs and created new work tasks. The retailer tried to respond by replacing humans in the jobs where automation could do most of the tasks and then bundling the remaining tasks and the new work tasks into new jobs but found this to be frustrating and suboptimal. For example, problem solver and specialist technician jobs were created to address issues that arose with the new equipment and to maintain it to the manufacturer's specifications.

Now we'll describe how the new work operating system—using deconstructed tasks—provided a better approach. The retailer used the new system to analyze each deconstructed task/activity in the pack workflow. It also used the questions described at the start of this chapter, allowing it to determine if a human, machine, or combination was the best solution based on the characteristics of each task and its value or objective.

Here is an analysis of each task, building on work in chapter 1:

1 *Pick up and assemble totes:* This variable, independent, and physical activity involves picking up a tote and assembling it. The objective is to incrementally improve performance for greater throughput. The work of picking up and assembling a tote is best done by a human, primarily because it is so variable and unpredictable.

2. *Associate each tote with a packing location:* The repetitive, independent, and physical activity involves moving the complete totes to an available space in the packing area. This work can be automated with a conveyor or with automation that "senses" when a space is available and moves the tote to that open space.

3. *Pull the labeled product from the bulk container:* This repetitive, independent, and physical activity lends itself to automation, which in this case is a robot arm that picks individual products.

4. *Scan the product label:* This is repetitive, independent, and physical work that can be automated with sensors that determine to which tote the product should be assigned.

5. *Insert/pack pulled product in appropriate tote:* This repetitive, physical, and independently performed task can be automated by a robot arm that drops the scanned products into the appropriate tote.

6. *Adjust/repack product in totes:* The objective here is to optimize space while maintaining the integrity of the product. This is variable, mental, and independent work best done by a human. It requires analyzing the products in each tote, reaching in, and carefully rearranging

the contents before another product is dropped into the tote by the robots in the previous step.

7. *Pull the packed tote, scan, and move to shipping location:* This highly variable work is best done by a human being, who can observe when a tote is full, pull it, and close it up. The human can scan the packed tote to determine the appropriate outbound dock and then place it on the appropriate conveyor.

Starting with the Work, Not the Automation

As we have demonstrated, the new work operating system starts with the work. In chapter 1, we discussed how our retailer first tried starting with the new technology to improve the performance of its distribution center and retail operations. Recall the suboptimal outcomes produced by this mistake (higher labor cost, additional jobs, etc.). Our work and research with hundreds of organizations reveals this to be a frequent outcome of starting with technology. Instead, by starting with the work, organizations achieve more optimal combinations of humans and automation by clearly identifying which human work will be *substituted* by the automation, which work will be *augmented*, and which work will be *reinvented*. The power of starting with the work is nicely illustrated by Tree Top.

Tree Top, a grower-owned fruit processing cooperative, provides fruit ingredients to more than twenty of the world's top twenty-five food companies and branded fruit products across the United States.[8] Contributing to its competitive market position is Tree Top's use of advance technology in its plants. At the start of the 2018 fiscal year, Tree Top embarked on a work transformation project in its plants with the goal of optimizing the use of automation. It was looking to automate highly repetitive, less technical work such as fruit checking and data entry to dedicate more resources to complex, more variable tasks requiring scarce technical skills.

Instead of following the typical approach of leading with the technology and then determining the work and human implications *after* changes to workflows and capital investments were made, cross-functional teams of HR, operational, and technology leaders led with the work. This involved thinking through work reinvention to determine which tasks should be automated, how work should be reinvented using a combination of automation and human talent, and where the work should be completed.

Only after these ideas were fleshed out were the engineers and technicians brought into the project. Approaching this project through a work planning lens at the onset resulted in significant production efficiencies as the team could analyze activities within the core processes that were being analyzed as well as adjacent ones and even improved the safety of some of the adjacent processes that engineers might not have considered. Through this process, the team generated ideas that could eliminate 5 percent of total hourly production work. As a result, Tree Top has changed part of its capital investment strategy to include labor optimization and process improvement ideas. After reviewing the revised strategy, the board of directors requested additional project ideas. When extra capital investment dollars became available, these were among the first initiatives to be funded. Operations and executive leaders now look to benefit from HR's insight and participation in other cross-functional projects.

Achieving the optimal combinations of humans and machines is never a "one and done" exercise. Indeed, the new work operating system explicitly includes perpetual work reinvention and reconstruction. That involves continuous monitoring, challenging, and stress-testing the work designs that emerge from it, which is essential to overcoming the inertia of legacy that will tend to pull work design back into a job-based system. This is particularly true with automation since it advances quickly, often in step changes from emerging technology. By starting with the work and not the technology, you create a much more effective foundation to optimize advances in technology. Starting with the work helps you better understand how the work supports the processes that lead to the end goal as opposed to trying to shoehorn the technology into the process and then force fit the work to the technology.

For example, in the retailer's distribution center, the applied automation was a variant of conveyor technology. It significantly increased speed, throughput, and productivity by improving product flow. Now consider an emerging technology disruption: social robots that leverage sensors, AI, and mobility to move around and physically interact with humans.[9] Traditional robots are limited to routine and repetitive tasks in one location, like the conveyor-based automation system used by our retailer, but social robots can automate routine and nonroutine tasks, in many locations. The traditional process requires product to flow from machine to machine or human to machine. Social robotics frees those requirements (think drones that fly, anthropoid robots that walk, or swarm robots that roll) by collaborating with humans in ways that were previously unthinkable. The robots' sensors allow them to evaluate their environment and the actions of humans around them, and their AI uses the data from these sensors to guide the robots' actions. The added robot mobility enables them to work alongside humans, resulting in significantly higher productivity for both humans and machines. However, such robotic automation also requires redesigning the work because automation now may substitute, augment, or reinvent tasks that were previously done by humans in the old fixed conveyor system.

Social Robotics at DHL Distribution Centers

DHL is using many types of work automation strategies.[10] Each strategy varies by context and fits different work profiles, space considerations, and infrastructure constraints. By experimenting and testing multiple technologies, DHL ensures it has a strong foundation for perpetually reinventing its work and creating a culture that enables such reinvention:

- **Follow me:** The follow me strategy involves an automated robot cart. The robot cart follows a human picker who controls the robot. Once all the cartons have been picked for that cart, the picker dismisses it and the robot cart autonomously travels to the pack station. The human picker waits for the next robotic cart to arrive at the pick zone. DHL believes it gets a 20 percent bump in productivity from reducing human travel time and that humans don't have to push the cart between locations.
- **Lead me:** In a lead me strategy, the robot cart leads the human picker between locations, displaying the items and quantity to be picked by the human and then placed in the robot cart at each location. When

all items have been picked, the robot cart travels autonomously to the pack station. DHL has realized productivity increases of as much as 50 percent with this strategy

- **Swarm me:** The swarm me strategy detaches the robot carts from pickers. Robot carts receive orders and travel to pick locations, where a nearby picker sees a task on the robot's screen and picks the indicated items, placing them in the robot cart. More than one robot at a time can go into a zone—a swarm of robots. As before, the filled robot carts travel autonomously to the pack station. DHL has realized 200 percent productivity gains from this strategy.

- **Holy Grail:** The Holy Grail is a mobile robot that can also pick items. The robot travels autonomously to a pick location, picks from a shelf to a tote, and then delivers the tote to the pack station. This technology, while promising, is still emerging because the robot carts are expensive, the robotic arms are slow, and the pick rates are too slow.

DHL lists five steps for testing and implementing new technology:

Step 1. Know your profile: No technology is a one-size-fits-all solution. To pick the emerging technology that's a right fit for an application, the first step is to understand your order profiles and peak-to-low-volume ratios, space consideration, and infrastructure limitations.

Step 2. Leverage the solution: Solutions that might warrant a bigger investment are those that can integrate with a warehouse management system and be leveraged across a network. They might even be flexible enough to move from facility to facility as the need arises.

Step 3. Know the point of no return: If you must make permanent changes to your infrastructure, you are probably stuck with figuring out how to make a solution work. Can we go back to what we currently have if the new solution is not successful?

Step 4. Measure all the results: It's important to understand the impact of a solution across all processes and not just a subset like picking or packing.

Step 5. Find the right partner: When it comes to a new and unproven technology, it is important to have a technology partner that understands you're not going to place a $10 million order on day one and who will support you as you get up to speed. Partnering is essential to managing the risks of new technology.

What if the retailer in our example had used automation designs like DHL? Then robots or workers would swarm to the product location instead of the product flowing to the humans/robots. How might the work be reinvented, and what might this mean for the physical environment and other organization systems?

Our retailer decided that indeed this "swarm" option was the most appealing next iteration. But how do you test it? Again, the four principles of our new work system can help:

1. Start with the work (current and future tasks) and not the existing jobs.
2. Combine humans and automation (not replace one with the other).
3. Consider the full array of human work engagements (e.g., employment, gig, freelance, alliances, projects, other alternative work arrangements).
4. Consider allowing talent to flow to work.

Following is how the retailer used these four principles to prototype swarm robotics:

1. What is the work? Swarm robotics could transform the entire workflow, but the greatest opportunity was in product picking. That was the most inefficient aspect of work and caused the most accidents.
2. How do we combine humans and automation? The current work of picking product involved warehouse workers taking an order and picking up product by hand or with forklifts and moving the product to the pack station. With swarm robotics, the warehouse management system would transmit the order directly to the robot, and the robot would move to the appropriate zone, where a human picks the product and puts it on the robot to be transported to the packing area. Now, work that was exclusively human before involves human-robot interaction and far less human movement through the distribution center.

3. Are there alternative human work engagements we should consider? The required specialized skills (operating forklifts to pick products) and the nature of the work (ongoing/permanent work with virtually no seasonal swings) suggested that a full-time job of picker would still be the best option, modifying that job in light of automation.

4. Does the new technology allow talent to flow to work? The redesigned job of human "pickers" was redesigned to allow them to flow to the work but not by moving. The robotics allowed the human to move the product to the robot that came to them.

Our retailer also considered some additional questions:

5. Can we extend the solution to our other distribution centers? The physical design of all the distribution centers was the same, and it allowed reconfiguring existing space to accommodate the robots and the new human role in order to pick consistently across all distribution centers.

6. Do we know the point of no return? Given the prototyping approach that underpins the new work operating system, the organization has immense flexibility in testing and iterating on the solution before widespread implementation.

7. What is the impact on the entire operation of the distribution center? How does this new solution affect other parts of the workflow? In addition to increasing the speed and productivity of the picking process, the automation would seamlessly integrate with the packing process. In other words, instead of viewing picking and packing as adjacent but distinct processes, the new automation would enable one integrated end-to-end process. Thus, the introduction of this automation would increase the throughput and speed of the entire operation.

8. What partners can help us prototype this automation? The retailer identified several different automation vendors that could partner with the organization to prototype the technology and iterate with it to ensure optimal performance.

While this was the end of the retailer's formal analysis, there is always a reinvention on the horizon so that the organization continues to monitor new developments. For example, as the COVID-19 pandemic has played out and restricted the ability of workers to interact with each other, some organizations have shifted toward "dark warehouses" that run with no human workers. JD.com, a Chinese logistics company, recently unveiled a warehouse that can handle 200,000 orders a day and employs just four people.[11] The four human workers' role is servicing the robots, with the rest of the operation fully automated. Thus, the warehouse can run "dark" (no lights needed for humans) most of the time, with only infrequent "light" periods when the human service workers are on site. The warehouse is part of a fulfillment center in Kunshan, outside Shanghai, that enables JD to provide same-day delivery to even the remotest parts of China. When packages arrive at the facility, they are immediately placed into a complex network of automated machinery, including fast-moving, automated conveyors and scanners that check the contents in microseconds. JD's smart logistics system groups the packages by region, and they are then sorted into large bins for each region. These bins are transported with driverless forklifts to the waiting truck for delivery to that regional destination.

Thus the work at JD has been transformed to remove all human workers from the distribution center and to create four regular full-time jobs that service the robots. Would our retailer be prepared for such a drastic change that might require the departure or redeployment of the current warehouse workers? The answer requires considering not only simply warehouse efficiency or cost but also how the current warehouse workers' capabilities might support redeploying to other work in the organization. It also requires considering the impact of potential layoffs and assisting the workers to find new work, topics that we touch on in chapter 7.

Deconstruction Applied to Knowledge Work:
The Talent Recruiting Coordinator

We have used the example of mostly manual work from the distribution center of our retailer as a running case study to illustrate our new work operating system in action, but the new system also applied to less physical and more mental work, often called "knowledge work."

For a large professional services firm, we reinvented the work of the talent recruiting coordinator. Recruiting coordinators are responsible for managing all aspects of a candidate's experience with the recruiting process, taking on a variety of different tasks. For example, they spend close to 10 percent of their time reviewing the application tracking system (ATS) to ensure candidate profiles are updated and all needed information has been uploaded. Recruiting coordinators then email candidates to request the missing material. This highly repetitive, independently performed mental work lends itself well to substitution RPA. RPA bots can continuously check the ATS for missing items and automatically email candidates when content is missing. RPA was also proven to effectively substitute for the recruiting coordinator in other tasks like offer letter generation and tracking and confirming start dates.

The impact of this deconstruction exercise was to identify that RPA could substitute for 42 percent of the work, comprising sixteen different tasks currently being performed by the five recruiting coordinators. The company redesigned the jobs to substitute RPA for these tasks, which eliminated all errors and significantly improved the speed of performing the sixteen tasks. What should be done with the time freed up by eliminating these tasks from the human workers? The recruiting coordinators now spend that time on personal interaction with job candidates and delivering a more personalized experience, work better suited to their human capabilities.

Conclusion

This chapter showed you why the new work operating system is essential to optimizing work automation, since optimal solutions usually combine humans and automation rather than replace jobholders with automation. We saw how the traditional system, based on jobs and jobholders, simply could not accommodate the challenges of today's work automation options, let alone the emerging opportunities on the horizon, such as "dark" distribution centers. The new work operating system reveals more optimal and nuanced solutions, but it requires abandoning the old job-based system, analyzing the deconstructed tasks independently, and then reconstructing the work tasks in a more optimal way.

Next we turn our attention to the options for engaging human workers, through arrangements that go beyond regular full-time employment. Once again, we will see that the traditional system based on jobs and jobholders is insufficient to reveal and act on the diverse alternative ways that humans may engage with the organization but that the new work operating system offers a solution.

A Checklist for Getting Started

1. Have you identified the automation compatibility of the deconstructed tasks?
2. What is the relevant type of automation for each task?
3. Unconstrained by the current process, how might you use automation?
4. Does that particular type of automation exist today?
5. Where can you experiment with emerging work automation?

3 Work Arrangements beyond Employment: A Democratized Work Ecosystem beyond the Fixed Traditional Organizational Boundary

There are justifiable celebrations about how quickly workers adjusted to the realities of the COVID-19 crisis. The most prominent examples involve knowledge workers adjusting to remote work, but even more interesting patterns were seen among workers in manufacturing, retail, and other on-site venues.

Deere & Co., the farm and construction equipment maker in Iowa, pivoted to making at least 225,000 face shields.[1] Maine-based company Flowfold, which ordinarily makes outdoor gear, pivoted to producing face shields, which required new workflows, materials, and training as well as getting product design ideas directly from frontline healthcare workers.[2] A custom outdoor furniture cushion maker in North Texas transformed in less than a month to make over 1,000 gowns and 700 face shields per day as a way to retain employees, who pivoted their sewing abilities to the new products.[3]

General Motors (GM), JR Automation (a Hitachi Group Company), and Esys Automation created immediate capacity to manufacture face masks.[4] The GM/Hitachi team designed an end-to-end production line, sourced and repurposed supplies, and transformed a GM cleanroom into a mask factory in only six days. Employees volunteered to transition from making automobiles to making masks, with GM filling thirteen shifts (315 people) in less than two hours. Sean O'Sullivan, employee volunteer engagement officer at GM Corporate Giving, said, "I sent out one email to the entire Southeast Michigan group of GM employees and everybody responded. A lot of our employees were looking to respond to COVID-19 in a positive way."

Some organizations gained agility by tapping new sources of workers. Stan Jewell, president and CEO of Renfro Corp., a sock-making company, pivoted to making one million face masks per week.[5] "The hard part" was finding 550 temporary workers to assemble and package the masks in seven locations. He solved it by attracting sixteen-to-twenty-year-olds not yet even in the labor market. He said that "what we really learned is that we're much more agile than we thought. . . . How do we use those skill sets that we just figured out that we're really good at and apply them in new ways?"

This newfound work agility also melts organization boundaries as work and workers flow between organizations. The Kroger supermarket company is temporarily borrowing furloughed employees for thirty days from Sysco Corporation, a wholesale food distributor.[6] Iowa State University's Center for Industrial Research and Service program enabled two companies located two hundred miles apart (Dimensional Group in Mason City and Angstrom Precision Molding in Ottumwa) to collaborate in making 100,000 face shields per week.[7]

Just as jobs are melting into more fluid tasks, conceptions of job-holding workers are melting into more fluid skills and capabilities. As a recent *Harvard Business Review* article describes, "The Covid-19 crisis has forced businesses in industries previously impervious to remote working to reengineer their work processes and bolster their technology support systems, which have been the traditional barriers to alternative work arrangements."[8] Job sharing, better known as *work* sharing "with a dose of federal aid,"[9] is touted by economists[10] and both US Republican and Democratic policymakers as a way to avoid layoffs. It uses state unemployment insurance to subsidize workers' wages so that they are kept on the payroll with reduced hours instead of being laid off. All of the former full-time jobholders share fewer jobs by working part time, giving the workers flexibility to take time off if they are ill or need to care for family members. Yet it preserves their relationship with their company, so they are available when conditions improve, and the company has lower payroll costs. Detroit enrolled 1,700 of the city's 9,000-member work force in such a work sharing program.

These justifiably celebrated and exciting examples reveal the important pattern we described in chapter 1, where work that was previously held in stable jobs is now "melting" to more fluid deconstructed work elements. This is happening not only through formal work design but often simply as workers crafting their work in new ways to address opportunities and challenges. What may be less obvious is that this is a benefit to the workers as well. They get to redesign the work to make the best use of their skills, identify where technology may be beneficial, determine reskilling opportunities, and see adjacencies between their work and that of others. Workers, previously conceived as jobholders, are now melting into more fluid or deconstructed capability elements (e.g., skills, capabilities). The talent pool becomes more ready to shift skills, apply nonjob skills, or move across boundaries between organizations.

Alternative Work Arrangements and the New Work Operating System

The new work system considers that work can be done by regular employees, but it also embraces the increasingly diverse array of alternative work arrangements. Engaging such workers requires work arrangements that go beyond typical jobs and the assumption that the worker will be a full-time employee who holds a series of jobs in the organization. There is a growing array of such alternative work arrangements, often called a "talent ecosystem." The list below is adapted from the Institute for Corporate Productivity (i4cp) and illustrates the most common work arrangements within such an ecosystem.[11]

Exchange talent with other organizations: Build capability, perspective, and relationships by swapping/rotating talent with entities outside your enterprise.

Gig workers or freelancers: Access on-demand skills and capabilities when/where needed using external talent platforms.

Crowdsourcing: Obtain input, information, and/or ideas from a curated audience internally and externally to the organization.

Innovation partnerships: Engage start-up organizations and/or academic units for new ideas, commercialization, or launching new ventures.

Co-ops/internships/apprenticeships: Use students and others who are early in their careers or are making a career transition to take on specific tasks and build a future talent pipeline.

Nontraditional talent: Source talent from traditionally undertapped sources such as underserved populations, different socioeconomic groups, and differently abled people.

Internal talent marketplace: Offer employees flexible opportunities to take on projects or tasks beyond their jobs to fill unmet needs.

Regular full-time employment in jobs should also be on this list, but it should not be the only option on this list. Rather, it should be one of several options that are optimized to best engage human workers. However, for most organizations, the list includes only employees in jobs. A good example of exchanging talent with other companies is the People + Work Connect platform that was conceived and invented by the chief HR officers from Acccenture, Lincoln Financial Group, ServiceNow, and Verizon and powered by Accenture.[12] It was invented during the height of the COVID-19 crisis, to give organizations with open jobs a map of the workforce available to fill them, and organizations with furloughed workers a map of the jobs that their workers might fill. The platform was conceived in March 2020 and by June 2021 was used by 265 companies from 95 countries and contained more than 400,000 roles. Key to this initiative was focusing on the goal of getting workers back to work and removing the traditional barriers that come when organizations perceive only their own workforce. A vital pillar was finding a "new currency," in the form of deconstructed "skills," rather than intact jobs. For example, the distribution facilities of a consumer goods company needed packers and pickers while an airline was furloughing baggage handlers. Though job titles differed, the skills-based approach revealed that the work of the two jobs matched, and the two companies could share talent across their organizational boundaries.

Optimizing alternative work arrangements, like optimizing work automation in chapter 2, is difficult and not optimal if leaders are limited by the traditional work operating system, focused exclusively on jobs and jobholders. Seldom does an alternative work arrangement simply substitute a new type of work arrangement for the regular employee in an intact job. Rather, the optimal solutions require deconstructing the jobs into their component tasks/activities and deconstructing the workers into their component skills/capabilities. Then each deconstructed element can be examined for its compatibility with alternative work arrangements, and the work can be reinvented and reconstructed to reflect the most optimal combinations.

Recall the three work engagement dimensions that we explored in the introduction:[13]

1. The assignment (or the work to be done)
    a. How small can it be deconstructed?
    b. How widely can it be dispersed?
    c. How far from employment can it be detached?
2. The organization (the boundary containing the work)
    a. How easily can the organization boundary be permeated?
    b. How strongly should the organization link with others?
    c. How deeply should the task involve collaboration?
    d. How extensively should the boundary be flexed to include others?
3. The rewards (the elements of exchange for the work)
    a. How small or immediate the time frame?
    b. How specifically to individualize?
    c. How creatively to imagine beyond traditional pay and benefits?

As we illustrated with the product designer role in the introduction, the new work operating system applies these questions to deconstructed tasks and worker capabilities rather than asking, "Can we substitute alternative work arrangements for the employees in our current jobs?" This focus on deconstructed elements provides a far clearer picture of the opportunities and challenges of alternative work arrangements.

How Alternative Work Arrangements Reinvent
HR Practices and Processes

Once you incorporate alternative work arrangements into the work operating system, the full array of HR practices and process must be rethought. Here are some examples.

Planning. When assignments can be dialed up or down on deconstruction, dispersal, and detachment, planning must now ask questions such as "Could we alleviate a planning constraint or dilemma by breaking up the job into its parts?" and "What tasks should be kept together and which ones separated?" Sometimes it will simplify planning because once you deconstruct, disperse, and detach the work to a gig platform like Upwork or Topcoder, your plan is simply to tap those platforms for a ready inventory of qualified workers on demand. Planning systems must design and consider options that include reaching into other organizations or consider what individuals would be willing to do the work as free agents. The entire notion of the "supply" of workers changes.

Attracting/sourcing. Traditionally, attracting, sourcing, and recruiting typically focuses on employment and looks for job seekers who want to work for the organization and who fit its requirements. The idea is to attract a pool of individuals for jobs. This requires a process of seamlessly engaging multiple systems (procurement, contracting, partnering, recruiting) to attract workers for engagements that may not be jobs at all. It's unlikely that any company could afford to have a job that involved developing advertisements to run on YouTube only during the Super Bowl. However, once you deconstruct that project and disconnect it from the jobs of the organization, you can imagine sourcing it with crowdsourcing or freelance platforms and rewarding it with a huge payoff or fame that could not fit into a traditional recruitment offer. The future head of recruitment must be as adept at attracting freelancers, volunteers, and employees borrowed from partners as at attracting candidates for regular full-time jobs.

Selecting. Traditional selection systems focus on choosing candidates to become regular full-time employees, often assessing cultural fit, and to make sure the employees have the potential for a career beyond their first job. When you consider alternatives beyond employment, the concept changes. You can choose workers for deconstructed tasks that can be done anywhere and paid instantly. Sometimes that means leaving the entire selection process to the talent platform. It's no longer as easy as saying "we select for this job" because the work can be deconstructed and reconfigured. The common language of work must now span everything from employment to contractors to volunteers. Will the head of "employee selection" become the head of "worker quality assurance" and be as adept at analyzing the selection criteria of platforms, contractors, and partner organizations as they are at selection candidates for regular jobs?

Deploying and developing. Deploying moves workers between different work experiences, locations, and assignments. Developing builds the capacity of workers through experiences such as training, experiential learning, and challenges. Thinking beyond employment means that work and workers move across a network of tasks, micro-tasks, companies, platforms, and alliances. Traditionally, development and deployment focus on promotions, demotions, and transfers between jobs. Thinking beyond employment means that these ideas give way to concepts like tours of duty, sabbaticals, special projects, and talent trades. The option to deploy work and workers across a vastly larger ecosystem than just your own organization offers advantages but also offers your workers vastly more options to chart their own learning and development paths. A world beyond employment provides development options to workers whether their employer provides them or not.

Rewarding. How should the notion of compensation and benefits change with the advent of a world beyond employment? The traditional mindset of pay and benefits for employees will evolve into a more varied and complex concept. Dispersed work means that even when there are tangible outputs, they are often created in one place and are then transported through intermediaries. This creates dilemmas for rewards that require personal contact to deliver. It also creates difficulties if you don't see the work until it is completed, so you can't reward effort, time, and/or motivation. When you're not the employer, some elements of what you can offer as part of the deal will evaporate, such as employer-based benefits and perhaps career paths and an affiliation with your organization. Yet talent platforms may allow you to entice workers with perks or offers that could not be made if they were employees, such as a big bonus for finishing a project on time because you know you won't have to repeat it for others or have to explain it to them. The notion of rewards slotted into an array of jobs arranged by hierarchy and market position becomes irrelevant when work is constantly being deconstructed and reconstructed and when the boundary is constantly changing.

For example, if your work system includes getting work done on a talent platform using consultants and by allowing trades and tours of duty with other employers, then what is the right "market" for setting pay levels and deciding what array of rewards is competitive? In today's world, these arenas seldom intersect, so perhaps even when an organization uses all of them, it's sufficient to say, "You are an employee, so your deal is different. Those Topcoder folks, the consultants we hire, and the people who work at the organizations where we trade workers are not our employees, so we can't incorporate them into our reward structure." Even today, such a position is rather tenuous, considering that Topcoder pay levels are fully visible, and the emergence of sites like Glassdoor.com, where employees anonymously review their company's management and policies, make it surprisingly easy for your employees to find out what others receive at other organizations.

When explicit connections exist between one organization and others, it makes the cross-organization pattern more predictable, so you can afford to create advanced rewards that actually capitalize on the permeable boundary. That's because if you create strong linkages with external platforms, contractors, or talent vendors that can offer unique rewards, you may be able to amplify your own reward structure through them. If you are the employer that allows your folks to earn extra money with side gigs on Upwork or other platforms, you can direct your employees to go there to get some of the rewards they desire and perhaps incentivize them to get the skills you need. If you set up a collaborative relationship with an outsourcer, contractor, freelancer, or platform, you may be able to induce them to deliver rewards that are beyond your ability as a single employer but also do it cooperatively with you.

Separating. The stage of separating is typically seen as the end of the employment relationship. It's traditionally an easily measured event that means ending the employment contract. Indeed, employee turnover is one of the most widely and well-studied phenomena in organizations, in part because it is so easily measured. Yet the notion of employee separation may be obsolete in a world beyond employment. The end of a project conducted by a contractor or freelancer is hardly a separation when that worker will be available in the future. A "boomerang" employee may depart to embark on a series of career stages in other employers and then return to the original employer as a more qualified candidate. Seeing this merely as a separation and rehire hardly captures the potential value of such a boundaryless relationship. An employee who leaves to join a consulting firm and becomes a contractor working with their original organization is hardly equivalent to the traditional concept of employee separation. In many ways, separation across the traditional organizational boundary starts to look more like movement between internal organization units. The greater the link with external organizations, the more options there are available within this permeable network. The more an organization collaborates with the external destinations, the more options there are to optimize the separation and return pattern.

Notice how, in the new work operating system, each of these changes in HR practices not only embody more work arrangements but that the optimal solutions also require refocusing on deconstructed job elements and deconstructed worker skills/capabilities.

Alternative Work Arrangements and the Retail Distribution Center

Let's return to our retailer. Like many organizations, the company had considered using alternative work arrangements, but the traditional work operating system got in the way. Given its legacy of seeing work as jobs performed by jobholders, this meant a rather limited use of a managed services provider (MSP) to provide temporary replacement labor for the packer job when employees were ill. Unsurprisingly, they found significant challenges with this approach as the talent provided by the MSP would need to be trained in all aspects of the job (which took away from productive work time for supervisors and other packers). This problem was exacerbated by the fact that the talent provided by the MSP could have varied from day to day, so the training would need to be repeated every day until the ill employee returned. In addition, there was an issue of governance as HR oversaw the employees and the employment relationship while procurement was responsible for vendors like the MSP. This split governance for work often resulted in significant inefficiency for managers as they tried to fill (temporarily) vacant jobs while balancing the potential flexibility and lower cost of nonemployee labor against the stability and predictability of current model jobholders in jobs.

By focusing on the deconstructed level, many of the dilemmas described above are avoided because the initial focus is not on replacing a job but rather on the more tractable and appropriate question of how the deconstructed tasks should best be done. Clarity at this level allows leaders and workers to envision alternative ways to reconstruct the work that can potentially avoid many of the dilemmas of the traditional job-based work operating system.

Using the new work ecosystem, the work is deconstructed into tasks/activities and the workers are deconstructed to identify their skills/capabilities. Think back to our questions pertaining to the assignment:

- How small can it be deconstructed? We asked this back in chapter 1.
- How widely can it be dispersed?
- How far from employment can it be detached?

For the second question, the organization has a variety of options regarding human labor. Should the work be done by employees in full-time or part-time roles, independent contractors, gig talent, volunteers, or third-party alliances or should it be fully outsourced? This is answered by the third question: how far from employment can the task be detached (even if it is performed on site). Can the task be performed on a standalone basis, or are there interdependencies with other tasks that suggest they should be combined?

After determining what tasks could be automated (see chapter 2), the retailer can now focus on the tasks most optimally performed by humans and consider whether a traditional job or some other alternative arrangement is best. These include the following:

Pick up and assemble totes. The deconstructed worker requirements for this task are physical ability, conscientiousness, attention to detail, and pattern recognition. These skills might easily be found in short-term workers, and the task might be dispersed and detached from employment. One might use gig workers or contractors from an MSP such as Manpower. The MSP is responsible for ensuring a sufficient and available supply of talent with these specific skills/capabilities, often in real time using very short-term assignments.

Adjust/repack product in totes to optimize space while maintaining product integrity. This task requires some judgment about how tightly to pack the product and knowledge about which different product types are too fragile to be closely packed. Experience with this task can build such knowledge and judgment, suggesting it should be done by workers who are not short term. However, the task is not sufficient to fill a regular full-time job, so it might be combined with other tasks, like the next one.

Pull the packed tote, scan, and move to shipping location. This task requires attention to detail, some physical ability, and attention to detail, but it does not require experience with the task. It might be detached from employment and assigned to gig or contract workers. However, the task happens in very close proximity to the prior task of adjusting/repacking the totes. The two tasks also share some of the deconstructed capabilities/skills.

The retailer's decision was to combine the task of adjusting/repacking totes with that of pulling the tote, scanning it, and moving it into a "reinvented" packer job. It would be difficult to detach any of the tasks within this "bundle," and the variation in the work will keep an employee engaged as it requires a diversity of skills to perform the work and there is a premium associated with greater experience in performing the tasks. With the two tasks combined, the retailer constructed a regular full-time job that was more optimal than treating each task separately.

The next question is how best to connect the talent to the work. Recall the three options we described in the introduction:

1. Talent in fixed roles

2. Talent who flows to tasks and assignments or projects

3. Hybrid roles that are partially fixed and partially flow

Some tasks were combined into the packer role and were done by regular, full-time employees. These tasks were adjusting and repacking the totes and then moving them to the shipping location. In contrast, recall the task of picking up and assembling totes, which requires worker skills/capabilities of physical strength and dexterity, pattern recognition, and basic knowledge of the products. These can be easily learned or reside in a large portion of the worker pool so that they could be done by talent flowing to the task either from outside (gig workers or contractors) or by employees flowing from other assignments.

The retailer determined that the work of picking and assembling totes would be best performed by gig talent. The worker capability requirements for these tasks meant there were minimal training requirements, but the few minutes of training required had to be delivered frequently as new gig workers arrived. It was important that the gig workers be not only sufficiently skilled but also highly motivated. So how do you best engage gig workers?

The organization tried achieving these goals with their MSP, which had thousands of workers with various skills "on their books." The agreement stipulated providing sufficient gig talent was available at the desired cost. However, the retailer soon discovered that the MSP was unable to guarantee a sufficient supply of talent, and the cost was much higher than expected because the MSP charged a 30 percent markup on the wage level. Also, as noted, the retailer found that even this expensive gig talent had to be trained for a few minutes whenever a new worker arrived.

The retailer abandoned the original MSP and tried using a gig platform dedicated to warehouse talent. Examples of such platforms are GigWorx or GigSmart. These have markups closer to 10 percent, which reduced costs. However, the particular platform that the retailer was using had episodic talent shortages and struggled to consistently meet the staffing demands.

The organization then discovered a unique win-win. It involved considering its employees in other jobs as a gig talent pool. As is typical with retailers, the store associates were often seeking more hours/shifts, but the retailer had been unable to accommodate them with work in the stores. In the legacy work operating model, the distribution center could offer only full-time jobs, so there was no opportunity to offer store employees jobs in the distribution center since employees could not hold two jobs.

However, using the new work operating system deconstructed the work, freeing the distribution center tasks from traditional jobs. This provided an opportunity for store employees to become internal gig workers in the distribution center. Because the store associates were already regular employees, they were more diligent and reliable than external short-term gig employees when they performed distribution center work. These internal gig workers also were more dedicated to the mission and purpose of the organization because they were also regular employees in the stores. The internal gig arrangement also removed the third-party overhead of using an external gig platform or an MSP.

The retailer built its own platform or "internal work marketplace," available to both internal (employees) and external (contract gig workers) talent. At first, the retailer used store employees as gig workers only as a supplement to workers from the external platform. Then as the internal marketplace became more familiar, internal gig workers became more plentiful. As a result, the retailer changed this model to rely more equally on both store employees and external gig workers.

Of course, having store employees take on extra work in the distribution center required attention to overtime pay and distinctions between part- and full-time work (such as when store employees worked more than forty hours a week when combining work at the store and gigs at the distribution center). The retailer responded by calibrating the algorithm that matched talent to various shift schedules to prioritize the elimination of this risk when selecting and assigning talent from the stores to various shifts in the distribution center. The algorithm would assess the total store hours for which each gig worker was scheduled and then assign them to distribution center shifts in a way that ensured they did not work more than forty hours in a week. As a store associate's store hours changed, the algorithm would recalibrate their schedules in the distribution center.

As you can see, the new work operating system, and our three criteria, more clearly illuminate the work and reveal a winning solution. The assignment of picking totes can be detached from a job but does not need to be detached from employment. The organization boundary can be permeable to an outside MSP, but the organization can also permeate the boundary between the distribution center and stores. The reward element remains tied to employment but is revised to pay for the tasks completed (or hours worked on a task), in both stores and distribution center, rather than paying for a single job.

The Impact of the COVID-19 Pandemic on the New Work Operating System

The COVID-19 crisis created new realities for gig talent flowing to work in the distribution center. Specifically, the pandemic exponentially increased demand for the retailer's products, which created more work for store employees and reduced the number who were able to take on gig work at the distribution center. However, the distribution center benefited from furloughs at businesses affected negatively by the pandemic, like airlines and hospitality companies. These workers became a new supply of external gig talent who were now available to work at the distribution center.

The pandemic also significantly altered how this talent would engage with work. Normally, gig workers would walk to pick up the totes, assemble them, and then place them close to the conveyor. COVID-19 protocols forced distribution center leaders to rethink workflows and the locations of both product and equipment to minimize human interaction and ensure sufficient space between workers. Gig workers were stationed in specific locations near the stacked totes, and the assembled totes were stacked in one location. Interestingly, this forced rethink improved the flow of work, reducing the number of bottlenecks. COVID-19 protocols have not just significantly changed work today; they also establish constraints for the ongoing reinvention of work and future automation considerations.

Patagonia is an outdoor retail company that designs and provides sustainable food and outdoor clothing to achieve a single focused mission: "We're in business to save our home planet." The company's products include outdoor clothing, outdoor gear, and organically sourced food and beverages using regenerative agricultural practices. The COVID-19 crisis reduced in-store customer demand, creating a danger of forced layoffs among store associates. However, at the same time, the COVID-19 crisis rapidly increased workload and worker demand in the online retail support center. Patagonia realized that a solution to keeping the store associate jobs was to let associates contribute to the accelerated online demand, particularly if both store associates and customer service representatives could now work from home. A challenge was that the two jobs were evaluated and paid differently, and there was little common currency between the jobs. Once Patagonia deconstructed the two jobs, it discovered that it could reconstruct the work so that many store associates could shift from one type of work to another. That presented issues on how to level the pay between the two jobs fairly and equitably. The solution was to reconstruct the work into a new job that contained the overlapping tasks and to just have that job's pay be the same, whether done by a customer service representatives or a store associate.

Optimizing Work without Jobs

What might a more extensive ecosystem of work without jobs look like?

A global insurer created an agile, global shared data science capability supporting its worldwide functions and divisions, extracting all such talent from the jobs they were in within other parts of the organization. The intent was to enable talent to flow to projects through the matching of skills to work instead of the legacy approach of matching a person to a position. The insurer first defined all the skills required in a data science function (e.g., knowledge and ability to use programming languages such as R and Python, Knowledge of Linear Modelling, etc.). All talent was assigned to a single job code in the company's system of record and a baseline for compensation was established. Actual pay levels were then flexed up or down from that baseline based on the market price of various combinations of skills possessed by the talent (e.g., someone with Python, R, and Linear Modelling skills versus someone else with Python, R, and Angular). The talent was managed as pools of skills and matched to a variety of types of work (projects, assignments, etc.). A new HR center of expertise helped business leaders design projects and assignments instead of opening a requisition for a new job as they would have done in the past. These projects were posted on the company's global internal talent marketplace and the machine learning algorithm underpinning the marketplace translated the work activities within each project into skills required to perform the work. The algorithm then matched the required skills with those possessed by the talent in the shared data science function. It also considered where talent may have adjacent skills to do the work, their interest in the work, and their capacity to take on the work. The algorithm also sent signals to employees as to what skills were trending up versus trending down in the marketplace along with specific upskilling recommendations so talent could continue to stay relevant in the face of the evolving work of the organization.

The cultural and capability shift required of managers to operate in this way is significant. The perceived loss of control and complexity that comes from having to get work done through a series of assignments and projects and not their own full-time employees in jobs required the organization to engage in some intensive change management. The change management plan included compiling resources to help managers understand the economic rationale for this model, providing support for constructing projects, and clearly defining outcomes and various tips and tricks for managing assignments. For example, to ensure that everyone working on a project whether they were in Mumbai or San Francisco was equally engaged and collaborating effectively, managers were asked to ensure that everyone participated in meetings virtually. They did not meet in a conference room as this had the effect of creating an "uneven playing field" and inhibiting full and equal participation, particularly in highly collaborative activities. We will discuss the implications for leadership, management, and coordination in chapter 6.

A sort of career progression evolved in this skills-driven marketplace, based on acquiring higher-order or higher-demand skills (as opposed to moving up from one organizational level to another). They identified high-demand skills not only as those demanded inside the insurer's organization but also through using data from external organizations like Burning Glass and EMSI to provide insight into the external demand for various skills. These two sources of data were combined to inform the data science workers about the skills they should acquire to stay relevant to current and likely future projects. The algorithms of the work platform also calculated gaps between the skills being offered by workers and the skills needed by the posted projects. These skill gaps were matched to learning resources, and those resources were recommended to candidates who were "almost qualified" to make themselves fully qualified.

This insurer's data science function illustrates how the new work operating system embodies an ecosystem of work without jobs. While the workers are employees of the company, they are not organized into jobs. They instead continually flow to assignments and projects. A key foundation for this ecosystem is that the workers are not seen as jobholders but rather as bundles of deconstructed skill/capabilities that are available for assignments and can be augmented as gaps are revealed. Workers are now treated as a more complete skill profile rather than only as jobholders. Careers can be more fluid because they are not limited by whether or not there is an available "next job."

Deconstructing Pay: From Paying for a Job to Rewarding Work and Capability

A key feature of the new work operating system is to match capabilities efficiently and effectively to tasks, beyond the tradition of a "one-to-one" relationship between a jobholder and a job to the "many-to-many" relationships between skills or capabilities and tasks. The new work operating system offers a new value exchange between workers and organizations that goes beyond traditional "compensation" or "remuneration" for jobs. It holds the promise of rewarding perpetually reinvented skills and capabilities instead of only jobholding.

Recall how data scientists in our insurance company were organized in a manner that allowed them to flow to the work. Should you create a hypothetical job for this talent and pay them based on the market value of like jobs? Or is there an opportunity to use rewards as a more effective tool by rewarding skills and work more explicitly? Building on our earlier analysis of alternative HR practices, the table below goes into more detail about rewards, illustrating some differences in the reward architecture under the traditional versus the new work operating system.

A key requirement is to benchmark the market price for capabilities, skills, and work elements instead of jobs. In the insurance company data scientist example, the data scientists were organized as a team that allowed them to flow to work based on the skills required to perform that work. How might we value the bundle of skills required to perform the typical work demanded of this team? Can we deconstruct the pay to reflect to the value of various skill combinations? Companies are increasingly using digital tools that analyze the market price of skills and make compensation recommendations based on different skill combinations. For example, we might determine that the median base salary for a data science analytics and business intelligence specialist in the United States with the five most common core skills (e.g., HTML5, AngularJS) is $120,000. What if we added C++ as a required skill? The tool might indicate that adding this skill would

Reward elements	Traditional work operating system	New work operating system
Philosophy	Emphasis is on highly competitive compensation to attract a critical but scarce skill set. Rewards are set annually or for a long time period. They are aligned with other jobs in the company to allow easier administration and internal equity.	Emphasis is on personalization and individual choice. Provides rewards for completing specific tasks at a specific time. It is aligned to encourage continued skill acquisition for future performance.
Compensation	Base compensation is primarily tied to the market value of the job with limited change for additional skill acquisition. Additional performance-based pay is typically tied to backward facing outcomes like achieving annual job objectives and company profitability.	Compensation is managed as a total pool as opposed to segmented programs with a greater focus on the forward-looking measures like growth, skills acquisition, and potential. While there may well be specific rewards for completing specific tasks or projects, the market pay level is set for specific tasks and skills, and total pay is the sum of those deconstructed elements.
Benefits	Benefits are collective and increase with tenure, premised on a long-term employment relationship.	Benefits are personalized and emphasize short-term choice. There is flexibility to frequently combine different reward/benefit elements (e.g., lower cash pay or pension contribution for higher healthcare coverage or more tax-advantaged "learning dollars." This level of personalization makes the organization more attractive to a much larger and more diverse pool of talent, increasing its ability to compete for skilled labor).
Learning and development	Learning and development is focused on preparing for future jobs in standard career paths. There are a broad range of learning resources but only limited guidance about emerging gaps at the level of deconstructed skills/capabilities.	Workers receive continuous signals about skill- and task-level supply and demand, and pricing, both internal and external to the organization. Learning resources focus on deconstructed tasks and skills and emphasize specific gaps.
Work environment	The environment is traditional, emphasizing jobs and jobholders, presuming a long-term relationship, and annual or long-term predefined objectives.	It is collaborative environment that connects talent from a variety of different work relationships (employees, gig workers, contractors, etc.) into networks that come together to solve specific challenges and continuously recalibrate to reflect changing internal needs and external circumstances.

increase the market price of the new skill bundle to $135,000. Tools like this are critical for both companies and individuals, ensuring that rewards (and labor cost) are aligned with the organization's shifting skill requirements while also helping guide individuals' skill acquisition/ development decisions.

Conclusion

The new work operating system encourages a focus on deconstructed elements of work and workers and thus reveals vastly more opportunities to engage workers in ways beyond regular full-time employment. Even for regular employees, the new work operating system allows more options and fluidity in how they contribute and are rewarded.

As we have seen, tapping such alternative work arrangements within the traditional work operating system based on jobs and jobholders is cumbersome and ineffective because it frames the question in terms of substituting alternative workers for the employees in jobs. What is needed is a more nuanced approach where each work task and each worker capability is considered independently, and then the logical work arrangements for each deconstructed task are reinvented to produce new work arrangements.

The example of the retail distribution center showed that when leaders tried to solve their work challenges by thinking in terms of jobs, they could see no way to create a job description that allowed store associates to take on additional work in the distribution center through internal gigs. Freed from considering the work as contained in jobs, and workers as jobholders, leaders realized they could design a hybrid combination of a regular job (store associate) augmented by internal gig opportunities aimed at the tasks (picking and packing totes in the distribution center) precisely where those opportunities made the most sense.

This chapter reinforced the fact that the new work operating system must not only deconstruct jobs to understand the work but also similarly deconstruct the workers to understand their capabilities. Tapping talent sources outside of regular employees makes this idea vivid. In the next chapter, we delve deeper into this important point by offering a playbook for considering the total array of worker capabilities beyond merely those needed for a job.

A Checklist for Getting Started

1. What deconstructed tasks might lend themselves to alternative work arrangements beyond regular full-time employment?
2. What is the best way to connect talent to those work tasks (talent in fixed roles, hybrid roles, talent who flows to work)?
3. What alternative work arrangements are available?
4. To which tasks is each arrangement best suited?
5. How should HR practices be reinvented to engage talent through such alternative arrangements?

4 Deconstructed Workers: Seeing the Whole Person through Skills/Capabilities versus Simply Jobholders

How should organizations and society account for the capabilities of individuals, workers, and potential workers? Traditionally, organizations attach worker capability to their job, and most HR systems operate by determining whether a person is qualified for entry-level jobs or new jobs within the organization. Training programs focus on preparing workers for jobs, and the work system tracks the jobs and job titles individuals have held. The traditional resume lists these previous job titles as well as education. Educational institutions traditionally account for learning by conferring degrees, comprised as lists of successfully completed courses or a particular "major." Putting the two together, the traditional work operating system constructs intact jobs with a set of qualifications and then searches for candidates that possess the proper intact degrees or job experience, rejecting those who are not fully "qualified."

Seeing work and workers in this way is a recipe for suboptimization in the face of the accelerated need for agility that we have described. First, when a worker's qualifications are embedded in a school degree, or in the job titles they have held, any capabilities unrelated to the degree or the job become invisible. Recall the example in the introduction, where automating retail store checkout would require laying off those with the job of cashier when in fact these cashiers often have adjacent capabilities that partially qualify them for the new work. A traditional work system based on jobs and jobholders cannot see the cashiers' adjacent skills. Organizations often refer to this as seeing the whole person as they adopt systems to map the full array of worker qualifications, only some of which will be used in any job but any one of which might become relevant as the work changes.

Second, as we noted earlier, the traditional work operating system, based on work as a job and worker as a jobholder, tends to create a myopic focus on whether workers are fully qualified for a particular job. Particularly in times of labor shortages or rapid change, the right question is not "is a worker fully qualified for this job" but rather "which potential workers are mostly qualified, and what would it take to make them fully qualified?" Identifying the mostly qualified requires a work system capable of seeing workers as an array of skills/capabilities rather than as a holder of a degree or a job.

Deconstructing degrees and jobs into skills/capabilities is a pillar of efforts by industry and policymakers to deal with some of the most vital talent gaps. As early as 2017, Ginny Rometty, the former CEO of IBM, was an adamant proponent of this approach. Rometty suggested these are "new collar jobs," neither traditionally blue-collar nor white-collar. In the United States. alone, there were more than 500,000 open jobs in tech-related sectors.[1] In a *USA Today* column, Rometty explained that not all tech jobs require a college degree. "At a number of IBM's locations . . . as many as one-third of employees don't have a four-year degree," Rometty wrote. "What matters most is that these employees . . . have relevant skills, often obtained through vocational training." As industries transform, she says, work is being created that "demands new skills—which in turn requires new approaches to education, training and recruiting."[2]

What are those new approaches? IBM intended to hire six thousand employees by the end of 2017, many of whom would have unconventional backgrounds. "About 15 percent of the people we hire in the U.S. don't have four-year degrees," said IBM's vice president of talent Joanna Daly. "There's an opportunity to broaden the candidates to fill the skills gap."[3] IBM also announced that it would be partnering with community colleges across the United States to better prepare more Americans for "new collar career opportunities."[4] For those without a formal bachelor's degree, Daly said she looks for hands-on experience and that enrolling in relevant vocational classes.

By late 2020, many more organizations had formally recognized this approach. For example, the Aspen Institute Cybersecurity Group announced commitments from sixteen companies to grow cybersecurity and high-tech jobs using these principles:

- Widen the aperture of candidate pipelines, including expanding recruitment focus beyond applicants with four-year degrees or using non-gender-biased job descriptions.
- Revitalize job postings to focus on engagement and the core requirements; don't "over-spec" the requirements.
- Make career paths understandable and accessible to current employees and job seekers, referencing models like the National Initiative for Cybersecurity Education (NICE) Cybersecurity Workforce Framework.[5]

"Our industry often uses the term talent gap when describing the short supply of cybersecurity workers, but that is misleading," said Corey Thomas, chief executive officer of Rapid7. "Millions of Americans have the talent to excel in security—far more than we need. But many don't know it. Rapid7 is focused on engaging with underrepresented communities to show them their potential in this field."[6]

Of course, actual systems are a bit more nuanced. Even in traditional work systems, organizations often track not only the jobs workers have held but also some system of more granular work capabilities, often called skills or competencies. Similarly, even traditional educational institutions are increasingly deconstructing their educational offerings, allowing students to drop in and out of the institution between employment periods and offering stackable credentials, which may add up to a degree over time but do not require a continuous stint at the college to achieve that degree. The U.S. Department of Labor defines stackable credentials as "part of a sequence of credentials that can be accumulated over time and move an individual along a career pathway or up a career ladder."[7] Thus, in the new work operating system, stackable credentials are deconstructed credentials that can build an individual's qualifications and move them along a career pathway to different and potentially higher-paying work.

Stackable Credentials: Deconstructing College Degrees and Certificates

Once organizations and workers begin to operate at the level of deconstructed skills/capabilities, it is inevitable that employers and students will look critically at the array of educational institutions (four-year colleges, community colleges, certification institutes, and so on). They will demand that those institutions also deconstruct their degrees and certificates so that the individual classes and certificates can be better seen and applied to deconstructed and fluid work. There are many experiments and initiatives along these lines. One of the most prominent is stackable credentials.

Thomas Bailey and Clive Belfield, from the Community College Research Center at Columbia University, describe such initiatives as one answer to the potential problems associated with giving certificates a more central role in higher education.[8] This system would allow a student to earn a short-term credential that would be valuable in the labor market if the student stopped out of college or needed to work full time. Then the student could return to college at the original or another institution to continue working toward a higher degree without losing credits. For example, an individual might enroll in a certificate program to become an accounting clerk, then enroll in a program to become a payroll clerk or business assistant, and finally complete an associate's degree in accounting.

They offer another example where a student might serially acquire certificates in medical insurance and medical transcription; these might then lead to an associate's degree in science and a career as a health technician. They note that such stackable certificates offer the benefits of marketable credentials based on a relatively small number of credits and have the potential to lead to higher-level degrees and more complex skills. The authors conclude that "thus, they do not act as a dead end to low-income or first-generation college students who face many barriers to success in college and who might benefit disproportionately from the short-term nature of the credential."[9]

The U.S. National Skills Coalition launched a Quality Postsecondary Credential Policy Academy to assist six states in adopting a consensus definition of quality nondegree credentials. A quality definition must be informed by transparent evidence of the value of a credential to meet the needs of employers, a public process that includes input by key stakeholders, and it must position the student to make informed decisions about their education and employment goals. They agreed on key criteria, including:[10]

- Evidence of substantial job opportunities associated with the credential.
- Evidence that competencies are mastered by credential holders, beyond fulfilling a standard number of hours or credits, but instead the student should demonstrate proficiency.
- Evidence of employment and earnings outcomes after obtaining the credential.
- Credential stackability, where short-term training for an in-demand job may be necessary.

We will return in chapter 7 to some of the policy issues necessary to make such systems more widespread and integrated. Here, we call attention to these initiatives as one example of how work and worker deconstruction in the new work operating system have direct implications for the educational institutions that prepare workers. The new work operating system is needed to address thorny challenges of connecting education to work, just as it is needed within organizations to address thorny issues of rapid change, automation, and alternative work arrangements.

A Common Language for Worker Capabilities

We see in these experiments the start of systems that deconstruct individual capabilities in the same way that jobs must be deconstructed into task elements. However, even these systems are often proprietary to each organization or each education institution. Increasingly, the new work operating system requires systems for describing worker capabilities at a granular level, with a common language across organizations. Suppose a company adopted its own unique definitions of sales, cash, and depreciation. It could probably make reasonable decisions about money internally, but financial markets would refuse to trade in that company and financial institutions could not move money between it and other organizations. It's the common language of accounting that wards off such a failure to communicate and allows money to move beyond organizational boundaries.

The new work operating system must increasingly support workers who move quickly from one organization to another or who never join an organization at all. Siemens borrows Disney's marketing employees to market its hearing aid for children. Freelance platforms supply hundreds of thousands of freelance workers on projects ranging from logo design to software application development to documentary production. None of those workers become employees of the organizations that engage them, so they are never mapped into the organizational systems.

Just as institutions can't trade money without a common language, neither can they easily trade workers without a common language. Workers can't move efficiently between projects and organizations, or even between positions within one organization, when the language of work is imprecise or incompatible from place to place. One of the most vivid examples of this disconnect can be seen in the military's descriptions of its vast number of jobs. Organizations from Walmart to Starbucks to the US government wish to hire veterans, yet the military language of work doesn't map well to private sector jobs.

The Department of Labor provides a website that translates military occupational specialties (MOS) into civilian equivalents.[11] Select the Air Force from a dropdown menu and search for "analyst" and you get a long list of "interpreters and translators." Search "leader" and you get a list of jobs called "architectural and engineering managers." The site also allows federal hiring managers to see a list of military occupations related to civilian job families. If you choose the job family "accounting and budgeting group" and the MOS called "auditing," you get matching military jobs such as comptroller and yeoman. But the Coast Guard job description for "yeoman" is "counselor and source of information to personnel on questions ranging from career moves, entitlements and incentive programs to retirement options and veteran's benefits," whereas the Navy describes a yeoman's job as encompassing a wide range of almost purely clerical and administrative duties. Not only is yeoman seen differently by the two military branches, but the language of the job descriptions is also unlikely to provide sufficient insight into whether either type of yeoman can do a civilian auditing job.

When organizations borrow talent, as Siemens did when it allied with Disney employees to market its children's hearing aid, they rely largely on the partner organization's language of their workers' qualifications and capabilities. When you get workers from an agency or consulting firm, you rely on their language to describe what the workers can do. Often, these organizations have a very different language for the same work, just like the different military branches.

There is change afoot. IBM's Global Workforce Initiative aspired to have talent move freely across global units and between projects. That required IBM's global leaders to adopt a common skill taxonomy to describe the work so that one region didn't define positions like "project manager" differently from others. IBM required all units to adopt the same common language based on about one hundred "roles." The company then required all of its external talent suppliers to adopt the same language to better connect the external supply to IBM's internal supply. The greater clarity about what work was needed and what suppliers provided saved millions of dollars through better pricing for external talent.

To be sure, this is no trivial administrative issue. If you fail to develop an adequate language for work, you will overspend or miss opportunities to optimize getting work done with workers beyond your boundaries. Some organizations have adopted LinkedIn profiles as their record of employee experience and capability, noting that employees are far more motivated to keep their LinkedIn profiles up to date than to update profiles on an internal system that only works in one organization.

Policy debates about reducing global unemployment and skill shortages often focus on creating more good jobs, yet a significant solution may be to create "good work" that lies beyond jobs, which requires workers' credentials be transportable. The World Economic Forum has adopted the idea of skills as the granular currency to describe workers.[12] While skills are not the same as capabilities, efforts to translate workers and work requirements into a common language of skills are promising components of a new work system that sees workers in terms of their array of capabilities and not simply as jobholders or degree holders.

For example, the Philadelphia and Cleveland branches of the U.S. Federal Reserve collaborated to study and map the paths needed for a worker to move from a low-wage occupation in one location (such as from a counter and rental clerk in Philadelphia, Pennsylvania) to a higher-wage occupation in another location (such as a sales representative in Denver, Colorado).[13] The analysis focused not on jobs or degrees but on the deconstructed skills that were mentioned in job postings for the occupations. The map is created by estimating which skills overlap between low-wage and higher-wage occupations, and which skills a person working in a low-wage occupation would need to add, to better match the skills typically mentioned in job postings in the higher-wage occupation. There is also often information about how to acquire the skills needed. The result is a tool called the Occupational Mobility Explorer, which offers an online and user-friendly way for a worker to access the study results and explore the map to move from their occupation and location to a higher-paying occupation and location.[14]

Similarly, the World Economic Forum noted that one in five workers is employed in the consumer industries. So, it partnered with Unilever and Walmart to compare the skills in roles where labor supply exceeds demand and many tasks are potentially replaced by automation (such as machine operator) with those in potential future roles where labor demand exceeds supply and fewer tasks are potentially replaced by automation (such as laboratory technician or medical technician). One surprising finding was that workers vastly underestimate their skills, and that AI assessment can uncover hidden skills, typically tripling the identified skills.[15]

Deconstructing work and workers into skills/capabilities is essential to such mapping, which will become more prevalent as the work ecosystem evolves. We will return to this in chapter 7, in our discussion of how public policy can better support this.

Confining work elements (tasks, projects) only to a job obscures insights and opportunities that are revealed by the new work operating system. That system can deconstruct and reinvent those elements. In the same way, confining human capabilities within a jobholder or degree obscures insights and opportunities that are revealed by a new work operating system that deconstructs those elements, allowing workers to reinvent their capabilities with a clearer goal and organizations to connect work and workers more dynamically and precisely. A new focus on worker skills/capabilities and job tasks/projects ultimately increases the efficiency and responsiveness of a labor market by transcending the current one-to-one relationship between a person and a job to allow many-to-many relationships, such as between skills and tasks.

Deconstructed Worker Skills/Capabilities and the Retail Distribution Center

Let's return to our retailer and explore how it matched the various skills and capabilities of the worker to the work. Figure 4.1 illustrates how the reinvented role of the packer was created as a result the introduction of the automation and the gig talent. It also illustrates the shifting skills profile based on the activities being added versus those being redeployed.

Beginning with the "work" category in the figure, the first five rows identify the tasks that were being redeployed away from the role as the new work operating system was introduced. Recall from the previous chapters that most of the tasks were redeployed to automation while gig talent took on the work of picking and assembling totes. Freed from some of the legacy work, the packer now had an opportunity to take on additional work. This included the newly created task of training the gig talent who would flow to the task of picking and assembling totes.

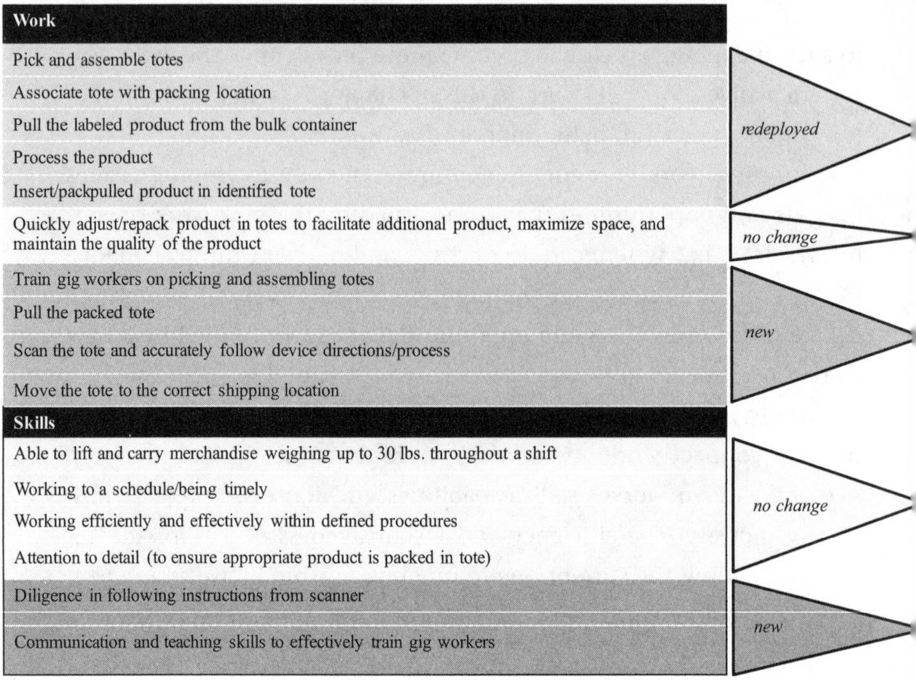

Work
Pick and assemble totes
Associate tote with packing location
Pull the labeled product from the bulk container
Process the product
Insert/packpulled product in identified tote
Quickly adjust/repack product in totes to facilitate additional product, maximize space, and maintain the quality of the product
Train gig workers on picking and assembling totes
Pull the packed tote
Scan the tote and accurately follow device directions/process
Move the tote to the correct shipping location

Work section arrows: redeployed / no change / new

Skills
Able to lift and carry merchandise weighing up to 30 lbs. throughout a shift
Working to a schedule/being timely
Working efficiently and effectively within defined procedures
Attention to detail (to ensure appropriate product is packed in tote)
Diligence in following instructions from scanner
Communication and teaching skills to effectively train gig workers

Skills section arrows: no change / new

Figure 4.1
Matching the deconstructed worker to the work

It also included work that was previously performed by the warehouser worker (pulling the packed tote, scanning it, and moving it to the correct shipping location). The addition of these tasks created the demand for new skills to perform the reinvented role, as you can see from the "skills" section of the figure. Deconstruction like this is essential to creating a clear link between work and the skills required to perform that work, unlike the opaque linkages that result from the more limited viewpoint of jobs and jobholders.

In the case of the retailer, no skills were rendered obsolete because work that was redeployed was replaced by other work requiring similar skills. Workers also learned new technical skills in the reinvented job. For example, knowing how to physically position a scanner and the meaning of the scanner signals were skills needed to operate the scanner and follow its directions. Also, more "complex" knowledge of the principles of effective communication, adult learning principles, and elements of a good work lesson were among the skills required for the task of training the gig talent who flowed to the work of picking and assembling totes. While the existing talent had the technical expertise associated with this work (it was part of the legacy role), the communication and teaching skills needed to train gig talent were new for this reconstructed role.

Once this pattern was understood, using deconstructed skills/ capabilities, the organization could match learning resources from its learning management system to the skills gaps identified. Learning resources included the following:

- internal online learning resources
- on-site in-person training
- bite-sized digital learning resources deployed to cell phones
- VR/AR simulations
- subscriptions to external resources (massive open online courses, learning platforms, etc.)

As we note at the end of this chapter and in chapter 7, when organizations and their workers evolve to the new work operating system based on deconstructing jobs and jobholders, it is common that they demand a similar evolution within the ecosystem of education providers, like the stackable credentials we described earlier.

Adjacent Skills in the Retail Distribution Center

In chapter 2 we discussed how the retail organization first tried to use its traditional work operating system by adding additional jobs (i.e., machine maintenance and problem solver) to make the new technology work. Chapter 3 illustrated the reinvented job of the packer, showing which tasks were being substituted, which tasks would remain, and what new tasks were being added to the role.

Now the organization could address the worker in the new role through the perspective of deconstructed skills and capabilities. Many of the skills required in the new picker role were the same as in the legacy role. However, there was one notable exception. Recall that deploying the task of picking and assembling totes to gig talent required training the gig talent. It was assumed that the task of training the gig talent belonged in the new picker job because the pickers were familiar with the tote picking and assembly work. Also, this seemed appropriate because the gig workers doing the tote-packing task would be physically close to the pickers.

Deconstructing the training task from the other tasks revealed an important insight. The talent in the picker job were comfortably performing most of the tasks in the new job. They were quickly able to learn how to operate the mobile scanner and follow its instructions. These "adjacent skills" proved compatible with the reinvented work. However, the pickers struggled with the task of training gig talent to pick and assemble totes. They did not possess skills such as effective communication, presentation, and emotional empathy required to train gig talent to perform this work. It was thought that such skills would be "adjacent" to the ability to do the tasks, but it turned out they were quite different from actually doing the work. The skills required for the legacy work and most of the new added work emphasized manual dexterity, working to defined procedures, and attention to detail. This training task had been added to the reinvented job of the packer primarily for convenience but without deconstructing the skills and capabilities to determine whether it was a true skill adjacency.

If the organization had created a traditional regular full-time job of "tote assembler," full-time employees would perform only that task with episodic training when a new person came on board. When gig talent performed the work, however, an untrained gig worker might have been performing the work every day, so training became an ongoing task. The nature of the work and its economics made it sensible to use gig talent for this task, even with the increased training required. The organization repositioned the training task into the job of senior packers to prepare them for to progress to roles of greater responsibility (e.g., operations coordinator or manager) where there would be a greater premium on communication and coaching. The company also developed online training to develop these communication and coaching skills.

Constructing the Logical Progression of Talent

In a typical work operating system, the jobs are neatly organized into levels and job families. For example, you would have an accounting job family within finance, and this job family would comprise multiple levels ranging from the chief accounting officer to an entry-level accounting clerk, with the levels differentiated based on the complexity of the work and the skills required. This job and reward-leveling architecture was designed and built for an era when it was common to expect stable and predictable promotion from one level to another, stable and predictable progression across job families. It relied on identifying the worker as a jobholder and the work as the job. The new work operating system, however, is predicated on the "many-to-many" relationships between deconstructed skills and work tasks in which skills are matched to a variety of work arrangements that range from gigs to tasks to assignments to traditional jobs. Recall the three ways in which talent connects to work in the new work operating system:

1. Talent in fixed roles with regular full-time employees, perhaps due to a convenient volume of work that fits a regular job or because of unique or difficult-to-acquire skills that justify offering a fixed full-time assignment

2. Talent who flows to tasks and assignments or projects, perhaps because their enabling capabilities are required in short-term specific bursts by several different work processes (such as a freelancer or project-based data scientist who moves between projects in marketing, HR, and operations as needed)

3. Talent in hybrid roles that are partially fixed because of work volume or skills dedicated to a job but who can also flow to specific challenges as needed (such roles often emerge from internal talent marketplaces where regular jobholders take on additional project work)

Our retailer used all three options. For example, the packer role is a fixed role with regular full-time employees performing the work. Gig talent from a variety of sources flows to the work of picking and assembling totes, while the senior packer is now a hybrid role: talent dedicated to the regular senior packer job but are expected to flow to the additional task of training the new gig workers as they arrive. Before, all the work was performed only by regular full-time employees holding traditional jobs. This new work operating system required rethinking the career architecture, with the new architecture shown in figure 4.2.

The career progression through the distribution center is now defined by deconstructed skills. This contrasts with the more traditional hierarchies that typically reflect either increasing spans of control or experience. In the progression shown in the figure, workers progress from repetitive, physical, and independent work that requires tasks like following a schedule, following directions, and physically moving products to work that is more variable, mental, and interactive and requires creative problem solving, analytical, and communication skills.

The tasks that are most repetitive, physical, and independent are performed by gig talent who flows to the work. Those in the gig role can progress to the full-time roles of the packer and warehouse worker, based on skills/capabilities. The next progression step is to the senior packer job, which is largely the same as the packer job except it now includes the task of training gig talent. This additional task, requiring communication skills and emotional intelligence, makes the role an ideal stepping-stone for the operations coordinator job. That job, with its focus on mental and interactive work, starts to place a greater premium on communication, analytical, and decision-making skills. The final role in the career progression is the operations manager job, with work that is variable, mental, and interactive and requires skills of coaching and feedback, critical thinking, planning, and communication.

Progression is now clearly defined by how the required skills build, so distribution center progression is more logical and transparent than the legacy approach, which was primarily driven by time in role and compliance with performance standards (e.g., product throughput) and adherence to work schedules.

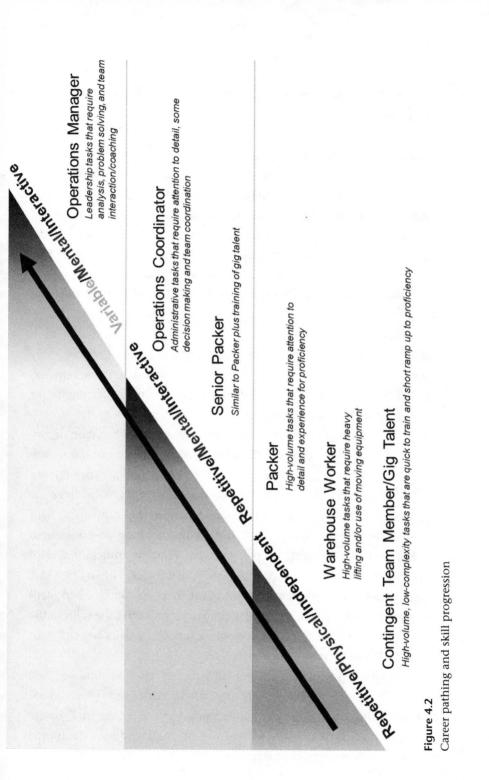

Figure 4.2

Career pathing and skill progression

Beyond the Retail Distribution Center: Deconstructed Workers and Internal Talent Marketplaces

This approach of matching skills to tasks is particularly critical to enabling talent to flow to work and is powering what is a growing trend among many companies: internal talent marketplaces. Such marketplaces enable talent from across an organization to engage with a work through a variety of engagements. Instead of the traditional model of moving a person to a job based on their experience and expertise, internal talent marketplaces match individual skills and capabilities to a variety of work options from projects and assignments to full- and part-time roles. Cisco's "one company, many careers" approach is an example. The company identifies the various skills possessed by each employee regardless of whether these skills are required of their "day job." That information is then made available on its talent marketplace, which allows individuals to find short-term "stretch assignments" or longer-term rotation assignments aligned to their interests.[16]

It requires considerable effort to create a marketplace based on deconstructed skills and work tasks. AI can help. For example, the Empath company uses machine learning algorithms and web scraping capabilities to infer the skills required to perform various tasks.[17] It can also infer the skills of workers by using AI to analyze data from the company's talent management systems, which tells it the skills that have been measured for each worker. Then the AI predicts what adjacent unmeasured skills the worker has based on patterns of skill adjacencies. The inferred task requirements and inferred capabilities can next be combined to identify gaps. In the case of our retailer, Empath would infer the skills of the packer and identify the gaps between each packer's skills and the skills required to perform the reinvented role.

The retailer initially experimented with gig work by limiting their gig work system to be an "inside gig," where participation was limited to those who were already employees and were thus "internal" to the organization. Typically, the worker will be employed in a traditional full-time job, and the participation in the internal talent marketplace will be in the form of "side gigs" that are undertaken only insofar as their regular job duties allow, such as in the example of the retail distribution center. Such internal marketplaces are an important and useful step toward deconstructed work.

Conclusion

Just as the new work operating system is predicated on getting real insight into work through deconstruction, it requires real insight into the worker beyond the summary headlines of a job or jobholder. By definition, the system humanizes the workforce as each combination of deconstructed skills is completely unique, allowing organizations to make more objective, unbiased talent decisions as a result of matching the skills to work.

The retail case study illustrated how the skills required of the new work operating system were defined and organized into a career progression. That skill-based architecture is also essential to enabling internal talent marketplaces that allow talent to flow to work.

Now that we have explored how you can engage workers as a whole person with deconstructed capabilities and best match workers to work, let's explore how you can both sustain and perpetually reinvent the new work operating system.

A Checklist for Getting Started

1. Have you created capability insight into the whole person through a deconstructed view of all skills and capabilities?
2. Do you understand the specific capabilities required for each deconstructed task and the gaps between those requirements and the skills of your workforce?
3. Do you have enabling technology to offer a continuous view of these ever-changing gaps?
4. Does career progression reflect the evolving skills requirements of the new work operating system? Or does it reflect other more traditional considerations like experience?

5 Perpetually Reinventing Deconstructed Work

When the implications of the new work operating system are integrated, you have a work system that perpetually reinvents combinations of deconstructed work elements, worker skills/capabilities, alternative work arrangements, and automation.

An Accenture report found that CEOs list becoming agile as their number three business priority. To compete in this fast-changing world, says the report, "HR will fundamentally reshape itself so that the function becomes a critical driver of agility. In this role, HR will enable a new type of organization—one designed around highly nimble and responsive talent."[1] Beyond being agile, HR must prepare leaders, workers, and HR systems for this new world of perpetually upgraded work. Leading labor economists and automation futurists have endorsed the notion of work deconstruction. For example, a PNAS article noted that "increasing a labor model's specificity into workplace tasks and skills might further resolve labor trends and improve predictions of automation from AI."[2]

All of these suggestions rest upon assumptions much like the new work operating system we have proposed here. They are possible only with a work operating system that can perpetually deconstruct, reconstruct, and reinvent work and workers at scale. This sounds daunting, but in fact we already work well within such systems when we use common products like the iPhone.

In *The Inevitable*, author and cofounder of *Wired* magazine Kevin Kelly describes twelve disruptive technological forces.[3] One is "becoming," in which products, services, and relationships are perpetually both obsolete and upgraded. Take, for example, the iPhone—as soon as a new one emerges, it's the hottest thing on the market and the old version dramatically decreases in value. This trend of "becoming" means organizations—and their talent departments—must be more agile.

The iPhone is an example of perpetual upgrades that are so common you hardly notice. Who could have imagined today's "phones" even a decade ago? The change occurred through small and incremental upgrades to things like cloud storage, application developer communities, integrated search, speed, AI, and hardware quality and reliability.

This pattern of incremental change leading to exponential differences is everywhere. Virtually all technology quietly upgrades in the background. If you opt out of the upgrades for too long, your technology no longer works. Once you upgrade one thing (your phone operating system), you must upgrade others (your apps). Eventually, you replace your technology just to keep up. For example, iPhone models starting with the number seven have no headphone jack, so wireless headphones must replace wired ones. Kelly observes that this is often heartbreaking and annoying: some of us really liked those wired headphones.[4] Yet as consumers, we don't notice how much we've already adjusted to perpetual upgrades.

Workers and leaders must similarly perpetually replace old work routines and habits, and over time the incremental change will produce exponential differences. Technology users learn to embrace perpetual upgrades that are both exhilarating and annoying, so leaders and workers must learn to embrace perpetual upgrades in work and work arrangements. That requires a new work operating system unhindered by traditional ideas that work exists in jobs, workers exist as jobholders, and qualifications exist as degrees.

In the 1990s, landline handsets were reliable, and they worked the same way for decades. This sounds a lot like good jobs that lasted decades and offered reliable rewards. Many in the 1990s rejected the iPhone, noting that it would require a vast community of application developers and massively improved computing power and storage. Today, some reject the idea of perpetually upgraded work because it will require a vast community of connected work providers, workers, platforms, and powerful cloud-based computing power, storage, and AI, just to name a few. But think about it this way: do you want to go back to using a land-line? Upgrades are never perfect, but the ecosystem has evolved with optimization frameworks and human and AI assistance. The parallels with work seem unavoidable, suggesting we will see the same evolution.

In your organization, there are likely already signs of upgraded work that is becoming something new. Perpetually upgraded work means that each day, the work becomes a little more automated, the source of workers becomes a little more boundless, the rewards become a little more immediate and nonmonetary, and learning becomes a little more virtual and community led.

Even after a more than a decade, few people use all the features of their iPhone, and in the same way, not every aspect of work will be upgraded in the future. However, as systems increasingly support perpet-ually upgraded work, we can now see solutions to thorny dilemmas, such as engaging talent when you can't predict the future, displaced worker adjustment, and work delivered "as a service."

Agile work is understandably daunting, and the path will not be per-fect, but it's a bit easier to imagine when we look back ten years at the "exponential" way we have adapted to perpetually upgraded phone technology. Incremental upgrades made us today's iPhone users, and incremental upgrades will create the future of work.

The new work system requires leaders, workers, policymakers, and the HR profession to prepare to be perpetually annoyed and exhilarated.

Sustaining the New Work Operating System

The traditional work operating system relies on relatively stable jobs and jobholders, and thus, relatively infrequent renewal and upgrad-ing of work and workers. Certainly jobs and job requirements evolve, but most traditional operating systems presume that once the jobs and their hierarchy are defined, they will remain, and a system can be built on that stable foundation.

So, the new work operating system presents significant opportunities but also a challenge. Once the system relies on units of analysis that are deconstructed work and worker elements, those elements are more frequently, and indeed perpetually, reconfigured and reinvented to meet new challenges. Workers begin perpetually crafting their work, using the deconstructed work elements, internal gig projects, and even external side gigs.

The challenge is to sustain this system when work is constantly evolving. The answer is not to attempt to capture the changing work in frequently revised job descriptions. A job-based system simply cannot keep up. Sustaining the new work system requires rethinking the goal to be one of supporting constant evolution while maintaining enough coordination and integration to keep the system running.

Executing and sustaining the new work operating system requires addressing five core elements:

1. Processes (activities and workflow)

2. Culture (collaboration, behavioral norms, etc.)

3. Talent (skills, capabilities, etc.)

4. Structure (organization of work)

5. Technology (automation, enabling technology, information systems, etc.) at scale

Underpinning each of these elements is the most essential ingredient of all: leadership. Focused, visionary, collaborative leadership with the capacity to orchestrate multiple work options is the engine that powers the new work operating system, something we will explore in the next chapter.

Sustaining the New Work Operating System in the Retail Distribution Center

Under its legacy approach, underpinned by the traditional work operating system, the retailer was limited to dealing with its various distribution center challenges using a typical job-based system. That would have allowed it to tie things like pay and benefits to jobs and to focus the work of HR only on jobholders and their needs. However, as we have seen, the job-based system simply could not address the changes facing it nor help it capture the opportunities from automation or alternative work arrangements. That meant that the retailer had to deconstruct the work and allow it to float between regular employees in the distribution center and retail associates taking on gigs in the distribution center as well as external gig workers. This fluid work, floating between several types of workers, solved many of the challenges, but it meant that the work was constantly being reassigned and reinvented between these three types of workers. That meant the retailer had to implement a system of constant monitoring, evaluation, and adjustment as the realities of the new work reinvention emerged.

We will now focus on a work plan developed by our retailer to sustain the management and engagement of internal gig talent, the employees from the stores who would take on tasks in the distribution center. Figure 5.1 shows ten tasks. They were first categorized according to their implementation timeframe: near term, medium term, and longer term. Each activity was then categorized by which of the five core elements it fit best: process, culture, people structure, or technology. Last, they were categorized based on their expected value and the potential effort required.

Let's explore some of these tasks.

Near Term (Six Months or Less)

Task 1 involved monitoring the work hours of gig talent and not violating any laws or treating its store employees unfairly due to misclassification. The company had designed the matching algorithm that underpinned its gig platform to explicitly analyze and avoid this issue, but the performance of the algorithm and the managerial decisions would require ongoing evaluation and improvement as the company learned from experience.

Task 2 was developing and improving the criteria for selecting gig talent. In traditional jobs, selection criteria often evaluate factors like fit relative to the overall company culture and technical competence for

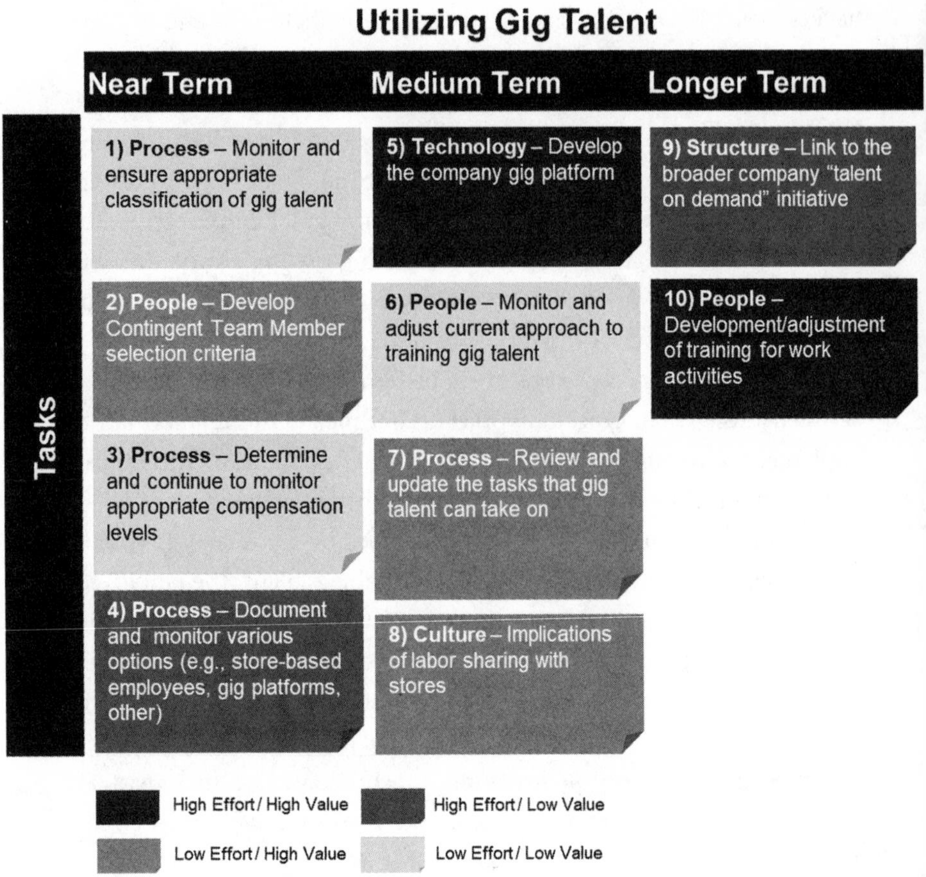

Utilizing Gig Talent

Tasks	Near Term	Medium Term	Longer Term
	1) **Process** – Monitor and ensure appropriate classification of gig talent	5) **Technology** – Develop the company gig platform	9) **Structure** – Link to the broader company "talent on demand" initiative
	2) **People** – Develop Contingent Team Member selection criteria	6) **People** – Monitor and adjust current approach to training gig talent	10) **People** – Development/adjustment of training for work activities
	3) **Process** – Determine and continue to monitor appropriate compensation levels	7) **Process** – Review and update the tasks that gig talent can take on	
	4) **Process** – Document and monitor various options (e.g., store-based employees, gig platforms, other)	8) **Culture** – Implications of labor sharing with stores	

High Effort/High Value   High Effort/Low Value
Low Effort/High Value   Low Effort/Low Value

Figure 5.1
Integrating tasks into broader organization systems

a job. With gig talent, selection is for the ability to perform a specific task, working effectively with their coworkers on a short-term assignment. Because the retailer had little experience with combining short-term gig employees with regular distribution employees, the criteria would be evaluated and modified based on their effectiveness.

Task 3 was determining and monitoring compensation levels. As we discussed in chapter 3, compensation for employees is typically benchmarked to jobs, reflecting job-based skills and market factors that change relatively slowly. In contrast, compensation for a gig worker is more short term and is focused on specific task performance and related skills. Compensation for employees might be determined annually, but it might be determined weekly or daily for internal gig workers, depending on the internal availability and the external gig market for the task. The retailer would need to develop a consistent and transparent process to determine and revise pay for gig work and ensure and communicate how it fit with the compensation for regular jobs. Again, because the retailer was new to gig work, this would require ongoing monitoring and improvement based on lessons learned.

Medium Term (Six to Twelve Months)

Task 5 involved ongoing technology development, extension, and improvement to extend to the entire company the technology that underpinned the retailer's initial internal gig platform for moving store employees to the warehouse. The goal was eventually to have talent flowing to work as a core feature of the retailer's work system, reaching beyond the experiment in the distribution center.

Task 7 involved continually analyzing the entire array of work in the distribution center to identify new opportunities for using gig talent. For example, it meant deconstructing the job of warehouse workers to find tasks in that job that could be assigned to gig talent. This would be an ongoing process as the retailer learned more about the capabilities of the gig talent and the openness to gig work among those holding the other intact jobs in the warehouse.

Task 8 involved ongoing enhancements to how much store managers understand and agree to labor sharing between the store and warehouse. Specifically, this meant the implications of talent from traditionally separate parts of the business interacting under very different work relationships and what that talent sharing might mean for the overall culture of the organization.

Long Term (Longer than Twelve Months)

Task 9 involved building and offering tools to the broader organization, equipping other divisions and functions with what they need to deconstruct their work, and creating the necessary processes and structures to enable internal and external talent to systematically flow to work. The distribution center lessons would inform a full-company "talent on-demand" initiative. For example, how might the lessons learned from using gig workers in the distribution center be extended to support functions such as HR or finance?

Redesigning Gig Worker Benefits to Improve Inclusion and Operational Effectiveness

As the retailer increased its use of nonemployee labor, a growing worker engagement discrepancy emerged. External gig talent was less engaged than the gig talent drawn from employees in the stores. Recall that the company had initially used an MSP to source freelancers working in the distribution center. To improve cost and availability, the retailer then modified the internal platform to source both outside gig workers and internal store employees looking to pick up an additional shift.

Over time, the retailer found that outside gig workers had a far more precarious existence than regular employees. The outside gig workers were therefore far less engaged with their work than the internal gig store employees. For example, outside gig workers had much higher turnover and absenteeism, which ultimately reduced the available pipeline for packer work. Further analysis revealed that the reason was gig workers had less financial security and poorer health and mental well-being. Outside gig workers were not included in the company benefits offered to regular employees, and so they felt they were left to fend for themselves.

The retailer's leaders decided that this situation was not only presenting very tangible operational challenges due to labor shortages but also not consistent with the company's values of community responsibility. It needed changing. The retailer designed a portable flexible account to which the company contributed an additional amount based on the outside gig workers' hourly wages (e.g., ten cents on every dollar earned). Outside gig workers could use the funds for retirement

savings, healthcare premiums or deductible payments, or funding training in new skills. This made the retailer a far more attractive option
for outside gig workers and produced a larger and more reliable a flow
of talent. The changes raised the cost of the outside gig workers but
increased longer-term sustainability and profitability.

How the New Work Operating System Underpins
a Human-Centric Culture

The disruptions of the COVID-19 pandemic (accelerating virtual work for
many workers and organizations) and global social justice movements
caused organizations to rethink work and their relationships with all sorts
of workers, including employees, contractors, and retirees. One question
is how to better ensure worker well-being. One answer is to add flexibility,
allowing more personalized worker engagement with the organization.
At the extreme, each individual worker might choose where, when, and
how they work as well as the terms and conditions of their work.

Some describe this as a human-centric organization, one that shapes
to fit talent versus shaping talent to fit the organization. This idea is consistently invoked in emerging ideas including the "reinvented organization,"[5] holacracy,[6] and "humanocracy."[7] Clearly, such human-centric
approaches require a foundation of the new work operating system based
on deconstruction. The traditional system of jobs and jobholders is incapable of such personalization and is far less agile than needed to respond
to changing organization and worker needs and preferences.

Human-Centric Work Reinvention at a Global
Pharmaceutical Company

A global pharmaceutical company illustrates the power of the new work
operating system. Even before the 2020 pandemic, the organization
had already established flexible work policies to allow some employees
to work from home and introduced diversity and inclusion programs to
support an inclusive culture. However, the pandemic and social justice

movements of 2020 revealed that much more could be done to achieve the goals of being a more flexible and equitable workplace.

Let's explore some of these changes and the perpetual evolution enabled by the new work operating system:

Schedules and locations are flexible. The organization had offered limited flexibility, including remote work limited to three days a month from home, no employees outside of the organization's main campuses, and all employees required to be "present" between 9:00 a.m. and 5:00 p.m. It aspired to more flexibility, such as unlimited work from home, employees located anywhere in the United States, and any work schedule as long as it included forty hours per week and met productivity goals.

How does the new work operating system support such aspirations? How would the company equitably compensate talent in different locations performing the same work? The solution was to determine salaries based on the market value for skills while applying a geographic differential to reflect the different local costs of living. By determining the market value of skills instead of jobs, the company was able to "personalize" compensation by recognizing unique skill combinations that might typically have been obscured when they are embedded in the market price for a single job or might not typically be available because they didn't fit any of the existing job descriptions.

Flexibility is extended to lab and manufacturing jobs. Before 2020, flexible work (e.g., choosing where to live, working from home or local office facilities, sharing work with colleagues across locations) had been available only in white-collar jobs. The company aspired to expand that flexibility to lab and manufacturing jobs (e.g., workers could choose their residence cities, lab workers could work in leased lab facilities at local universities, and manufacturing workers could share shifts and jobs through part-time schedules). The new work operating system ensured no decline in manufacturing productivity with such flexibility. An algorithm worked at the task level to integrate production requirements with requested worker flexibility arrangements, calculate each worker's optimum schedule, and recommend whether supervisors should approve, modify, or deny each worker's request.

Flexible work arrangements offer more options and can be changed. In the old system, work relationships were limited to either full- or part-time employees or independent contractors, and no movement was allowed between each category. The aspiration was to offer more options (temporary, job sharing, freelancing, gigs, etc.) and to make it easier to move between categories. For example, full-time employees might temporarily move to a part-time job share, or retirees could take on gig projects and shift to fixed-term contracts. This increased flexibility required a new approach to work planning. It also required planning talent requirements at the task level and using data-based triggers to predict change requests in work engagements. Simulation modeling predicted the impact of different potential work arrangements on organization performance and productivity.

A culture of inclusion extends beyond the walls of the organization. The racial justice movement in the United States prompted much soul searching in the organization as it considered both its own culture and its impact on the communities in which it operated. As it questioned every aspect of its legacy, the organization looked at both these issues through the eyes of its minority employees and candidates and the marginalized members of its communities. How could this new approach to flexible work contribute? The new work operating system allowed the company to become more attractive to a more diverse population of skilled talent who were not well represented in some of its operating locations. The new flexible work design and arrangements were often more compatible with this talent pool than relying on the old system of intact jobs. As these new diverse workers joined the organization, it became apparent that other changes were possible to make the organization more inclusive. The organization developed new continual listening processes to ensure that the more inclusive group of workers' voices were reflected in its code of conduct and values. It established a commitment making every worker responsible for living the organization values everywhere and at all times.

Social upheaval creates opportunities that exceed the capabilities of the traditional work operating system. The new work operating system offers a better platform to address evolving productivity challenges and opportunities as well as the increasing environmental, social, and governance challenges from the external context by continually recalibrating work and the organization.

Calculating the Total Cost of Work in the New Work Operating System

The cost of work must now focus on job elements and include work engagements beyond regular full-time employment. The new work operating system also requires that the cost of work includes technology that replaces or augments human work. This means capturing the cost of all types of work options (e.g., employees, gig workers, outsourced labor) on a like-for-like basis through a measure like the total cost of work (TCoW), as illustrated in figure 5.2.[8]

TCoW is defined as total labor cost (e.g., full-time employees, free agents, gig workers) + vendor cost (e.g., outsourcing cost, AI and robotics vendor cost) + annualized capital charge for relevant capitalized investments (e.g., company-developed AI or robotics, equity stakes in third-party work options). It is important to put all work options on a comparable basis so that the analysis is not distorted by differences in accounting treatment (e.g., labor cost is expensed, while the investment in robotics is capitalized). One should multiply the company's

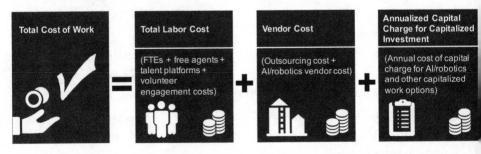

Figure 5.2
Total cost of work

cost of capital by the total capital investment in work options like AI/ robotics and alliances so as to capture the annualized charge for using these options.

The data to calculate these measures is readily available but is captured by different functions: HR might have the employee data, procurement might have the free agent and vendor data, corporate strategy might have the information on alliances, and finance might have the information on capitalized automation.

It is important not to let the pursuit of perfection be an obstacle to useful metrics. Orders of magnitude and a comprehensive view are the goals, not high degrees of precision.

Conclusion

The traditional work operating system is underpinned by a set of legacy jobs and jobholder qualifications and is often predicated on the assumption that those jobs will remain stable, and the objective is to make work and workers conform to them. Recall how our retailer first attempted to shoehorn technology and gig workers into traditional jobs and to manage nontraditional workers with its legacy job-based infrastructure of planning, selecting/sourcing, rewarding, and so on. The new work operating system is grounded in perpetual reinvention. The core elements of process, culture, people, structure, and technology are in perpetual motion as work changes, which both sustains the current way of working and pivots flexibly as work is reinvented.

A Checklist for Getting Started

1. Have you established a language of deconstructed tasks and capabilities to describe the work?
2. Have you explicitly considered how your process, culture, people, structure, and technology must change support perpetual work reinvention?

3. Have you provided technology and work coordination tools that allow the deconstructed elements to be easily recombined as demands change?

4. Have you reinvented your work systems (pay, benefits, sourcing, development, performance, etc.) to support perpetual reinvention and alternative work arrangements?

5. Have you revised your measures of work cost and productivity to capture perpetual reinvention?

6 Management, Leadership, and Deconstructed Work Coordination: Collaborative Hubs, Teams, Projects, and Agile Work Innovation versus Hierarchy, Structure, Jobs, and Stable Authority

The new work operating system raises concerns that it will encounter resistance and confusion from leaders, managers, and workers. For example, one leader who reviewed an early draft of this book said:

> I used to have four people in boxes called jobs with reporting lines that ran to my box, and I could call on any or all of them to get things done within the mission of our collective job boxes. Now, your new work operating system will dissolve the boxes, and my people become visible to other leaders through their deconstructed capabilities and will be available for their deconstructed tasks or projects. When another leader has a task that matches the capabilities of someone that reports to me, how will we coordinate the assignment? How do I decide when to allow one of 'my' direct reports to work on a task for someone else? How do I justify keeping them without appearing to hoard them? How should I take account of the desires of the worker either to consent or not to the request of the other leader?

Another said that "the iteration and reconstruction of work into new roles and projects requires that a leadership class of employees is always re-prioritizing and comfortable to break up teams and reconfigure them. Currently, it is easier for a leader simply to give her team members new priorities, as they are direct reports and aligned to her outcomes. But if instead these team members are transitory and pursue work activities and capabilities, then pivoting quickly could be challenging, and could involve negotiating with other leaders to free up their team members."

One might imagine several ways that these dilemmas might be resolved:

1. Let the leaders work out the talent trades through personal negotiation.

2. Let the workers choose the work based on their assessment of its attractiveness and developmental value.

3. Let transfer pricing or client value create an economic optimized marketplace (such as the consulting project lead who can bill the highest rate gets the talent).

4. Let algorithms optimize workload (like automated calendaring apps that now optimize meeting times) and just assign it to the worker (so when you arrive you have a schedule of tasks that were set by the algorithm, and those change every day or hour based on new optimization solutions).

Undoubtedly, organizations will approach the new work operating system with a combination of these approaches as well as others. The solutions will vary with the context of each organization. In this chapter, we don't claim to have the complete answer, but we will describe the issue and the potential options as well as the necessary learning and decision frameworks to optimize these options and their combinations.

Work Design as Agile Innovation

John Boudreau and Pete Ramstad suggested that an overarching principle for future work design should be to approach it as you would agile innovation.[1] They suggested this principle in 2021, when vaccines for COVID-19 became available. At that time, many organizations approached the question of optimizing the "return to work" as a search for policies. Their answers were as varied as "work from home forever" to "everyone must be co-located on site to achieve collaboration" to "between two and five days a week, with decisions made in discussion with your supervisor." Boudreau and Ramstad noted that many organizations sought "equity" through "equal treatment," requiring the same arrangements for everyone, and that this likely optimized work for no one.

Boudreau and Ramstad's observations were in the context of COVID-19, but they apply equally well to the dilemmas and opportunities facing organizations and leaders as work shifts toward the new work operating system. Instead of a search for one consistent policy, they suggested a policy: *"We can't predict the future of work.* However, we know that all of you have learned to innovate continually, as you have crafted your work to meet the recent unprecedented opportunities and challenges of the pandemic. So, instead of one policy applied to everyone, our 'policy' will be to *invite and equip you to design your work through agile innovation and experimentation."*[2] Existing agile innovation frameworks follow principles such as Experiment, Fail Fast, Learn from Failure, Don't Kill Questions/Ideas Too Early, and See Challenges to the Status Quo as Opportunities. They include practical processes such as sprints, scrums, and hackathons. The Genentech case study in chapter 1 described how the organization used deconstruction to deliver on a similar aspiration.

What could be more inclusive than welcoming new and different ideas about *work*—the thing that workers arguably know the most about and matters most to them? What could demonstrate leadership empathy, openness, and shared accountability more than to give workers a true voice in how their work is designed?

We have often found it useful to retool the way leaders think about work, organization, and people by reframing the issues through the lens of an accepted framework from other disciplines.[3] In this case, reframing is retooling work design through the lens of agile innovation. Organizations would ask where they already have frameworks for agile innovation, such as product development, marketing, and digital transformation. Then they would use those frameworks focused on "work design."

Existing agile innovation hubs equip leaders with tools for nurturing lots of ideas while keeping a focus on the overall goal. They equip workers with the freedom and opportunity to ask tough questions, challenge accepted wisdom, listen, translate the voice of customers into new ideas, and fail productively. They celebrate the innovations that fail, understanding that's necessary to find the ones that are truly transformative. The new work operating system will thrive best by applying these same ideas to work design.

Consider that some organizations' return-to-work plans include phrasing such as "we need HR to help leaders deal with employee complaints by explaining why our system requires that they give up some flexibility as we return to work." If we retool this using the agile innovation framework, it is quite similar to the old-fashioned view of customer complaints: "We need customer service associates to deal with customer complaints by explaining why our product or service can't be changed for them." Today, virtually any agile innovation framework includes rethinking customer complaints as "opportunities for innovation" and changing the culture and mindset accordingly. The same approach could apply to employee complaints about work.

The new work operating system will increase the amount and frequency of work design through more continual deconstruction and reconstruction. As with any continuous improvement process, this will produce outcomes with a wide range of effectiveness. Frustration is inevitable and even desirable. However, if such frustration is seen as complaining through the lens of the traditional work operating system, much of the potential for the new work operating system will be lost, just as defining customer suggestions as complaints squanders much of the potential value in customer ideas for product improvement.

Of course, work design is far more personal for your employees than the design of products/services, manufacturing processes, and so on. For example, an employee or leader whose has invested in a home or lifestyle that favors remote work will perhaps be less objective about work design than if they were on an agile innovation team designing a new product. Agile work design needs to account for a diverse array of worker views, ideas, and suggestions from some workers who may not traditionally have been offered a strong voice, newer workers who have not yet gained prominence, or even future workers whose voices have yet to be heard. Indeed, it seems promising to consider your current and future workers as the customers for your organization's work design innovations.

Not Chaos: Targeted and Logical Agile Experimentation

Does this mean unleashing a chaotic upheaval where everyone's work is now uncertain and subject to a radical redesign? No. Organizations already have tools that target agile innovation where it is most strategically pivotal and help determine where innovation is justified and where it is not. For example, when innovating in product/service design, organizations choose to experiment with certain features in a "controlled" part of their product/service or perhaps in certain markets where the costs of mistakes are less. The other parts of the product and markets remain stable so that the organization can keep selling products even as they innovate. However, even the parts of the product/service that are not actively experimenting can still pursue elements of agile innovation, such as gathering and evaluating suggestions for improvement and using analytics to identify potential system flaws.

The best approach to innovation is a systemic assessment to identify where the benefits of agile innovation outweigh the costs. As innovation proceeds, that balance changes because the costs of agile innovation go down as practice increases. The same is true for agile innovation in work design.

Can HR Lead Agile Innovation in Work Design?

As with all agile innovation, top leaders must ultimately be accountable. Still, agile innovation is typically executed by line or functional leaders in their own units. In applying agile innovation in areas such as operations, product development, and marketing, the role of the functions such as finance, legal, IT, and even HR is generally limited to participating as a supporting "business partner" with their client groups.

However, work exists everywhere in your organization, and so agile innovative work design doesn't easily fit in one arena like product, manufacturing, operations, or research and development. What function or discipline *should* lead and drive agile innovation in work design? This is your opportunity to challenge the chief human resources officer

(CHRO) and HR to expand beyond their traditional role as a supporting partner to the business units. Instead, HR can become a hub for agile experimentation and learning applied to work design. Rather than HR taking the role of explaining or enforcing policies and ensuring compliance, HR could be accountable for the organization-wide approach to agile innovation in work design.

HR would develop agile tools and frameworks, collaborating with your agile innovation experts to modify existing successful tools and apply them to work design. HR would lead in equipping and training managers and their workers to apply agile design tools to work design and to evaluate and monitor results. It would become the repository for lessons learned in targeted experiments and be accountable for integrating and translating those lessons for the entire organization. HR would also develop and constantly improve your frameworks and resources to support a system for agile innovation in work design, including what work means, where and when work is done, and how work value is created and shared among organizations, workers, and society. This is "agile work innovation," which spans your entire organization, supported by your HR.

The Consulting Firm Model

For many leaders, the new work operating system conjures images of a consulting firm, where the consultants move between projects and flow to the work as projects ebb and flow. What are the approaches, issues, and lessons from consulting firms? Consulting firms typically use one of two approaches: the first approach assigns a person full time to a project from its inception to end, with projects typically lasting for longer than six months. This approach is closer to the traditional work operating system, with stable and intact assignments.

The second approach distributes parts of a person's time to several short-term projects simultaneously. For example, an HR consultant might be working on the design of a new job architecture for one organization while helping another design a pay-for-performance program.

The defining features and distinctions between the two approaches, described below, offer useful lessons about today's approach to the new work operating system.

Project staffing/coordination. In both approaches, a dedicated staffing coordinator is typically responsible for determining which consultant is assigned to a particular project, based on factors like availability, skills, development needs, client location, and industry focus. The staffing coordinator is accountable for ensuring that talent is assigned to projects based on objective factors rather than on the subjective preferences of the partner who sold the project or on other factors that might not account for the broader context, across all available projects and considerations.

Companies in other industries would benefit from having dedicated coordinators as talent increasingly flows to work in the new operating system. Leaving work coordination in the hands of managers, as is the typical practice in the traditional work operating system, creates many obstacles (e.g., reduced mobility of talent and lower levels of productivity as work is organized into jobs that often don't fully use the talent's full capability or capacity).

Supervision. In both approaches, consultants are typically assigned to partners or managers who are responsible for their growth and development for a period of one to several years. These managers are typically in the same business unit or industry group that is the primary "home" to the consultant, but the manager may seldom work with the consultant on a particular project. Again, this is another practice that might benefit companies in other industries. Having supervisors who are focused on coaching and advocacy instead of monitoring and control, as is the typical focus of a manager in the traditional work operating system, can result in much greater worker engagement.

Performance and developmental feedback. The two approaches vary in the frequency and nature of feedback. When firms dedicate consultants full time to longer projects, extensive feedback is provided by the project manager, other consultants, and members of the client team at the end of each project. When firms assign consultants part time to shorter projects, feedback is provided by the lead consultant on each project as it concludes. However, the feedback is typically less detailed than is the case with the longer projects. Feedback from peers is typically sought annually as part of the performance review. Client feedback is similarly gathered annually and is aggregated to reflect the firm's performance over multiple projects. Thus, in the short project model, there is typically a much looser link between an associate's performance on a particular project and feedback from peers or clients. Having feedback and development directly tied to the work as it happens is another practice from which companies in other industries could benefit. The typical performance management process in the traditional work operating system is often an administrative process tied to administering compensation with only a tenuous connection to how the work is performed.

Remuneration/compensation/rewards. Again, the two approaches differ here. When consulting firms dedicate staff to one project for its duration, compensation (salary increase, bonus, equity grants, etc.) is significantly determined by project feedback in addition to achievement of goals like revenues generated and time billed. This is not the case with the shorter project model. The greater number of projects that an associate will have worked on in any given year requires that project feedback factors only loosely in compensation decisions. Instead, overall individual goal achievement is the primary consideration. The strong tie between pay and work performance that characterizes the dedicated staffing model could be a template for all companies.

How the Consulting Firm Model Might Evolve in the Future Work Operating System

The short-term assignment consulting approach more closely reflects the elements of the new work operating system, based on deconstructed work elements, but both systems offer helpful perspectives. One general conclusion is that even consulting firms typically rely primarily on a very human optimization system, in the form of a project coordinator to oversee and optimize assignments and a dedicated manager/mentor to attend to the goals, development, rewards, and well-being of the individual consultant.

How might this system change as the new work operating system evolves?

Project staffing/coordination. The new work operating system would suggest that both approaches will likely deconstruct projects into more granular interdependent and independent tasks. Similarly, consulting talent will be represented by a more granular deconstructed set of attributes and preferences. Rather than relying so much on human coordinators, AI and machine learning will take on the more repetitive and noncognitive work of matching deconstructed consultant attributes to a project's tasks and client characteristics. Human coordinators will evolve to take on higher-level work such as interpersonal negotiations between client managers who desire capabilities from the same consultants and interpersonal guidance and counseling to the consultants' supervisors.

Supervision. Instead of supervisors dedicated to the consultant, independent of the project, the new work operating system will shift supervision to the managers of the individual projects. The automated work platform would serve the role of today's consultant-dedicated supervisors by aggregating information about each consultant on each project in real time. Thus the platform would provide subsequent project managers with the consultant's strengths, development opportunities, interests, and so on while AI would be monitoring each consultant's performance and progress, recommending alternative career pathways for growth and recommending various skill acquisition opportunities based on interest and need. Human project managers can then focus their efforts on directly coaching the consultant over the course of the project.

Performance and developmental feedback. Feedback will be much more frequent and less time consuming. Consultants will receive frequent "bite-sized chunks" of feedback over the course of both long and short projects. AI will aggregate these bite-sized chunks into a more comprehensive end of project review, prompting colleagues and consultants to modify the feedback.

Remuneration/compensation/rewards. Instead of year-end compensation reviews, which typically have very weak links to individual project performance or outcomes, compensation will be tied to performance on project tasks. Rewards will be paid and adjusted after each project, based on project performance and whether the acquired skills are those being demanded by clients or critical to performing well on future projects. Instead of being paid once annually, bonuses will be paid at the end of each project. Annual salary increases and equity grants would be determined based on the skills acquired over the course of the year and how pivotal those skills are to meeting future client needs.

The common challenges in this newly evolved consulting firm work operating system would be the following:

1. Equipping managers to deconstruct roles and post tasks instead of opening a requisition for a new job

2. Manager capability in organizing projects, monitoring work quality, and so on

3. Getting employees to post skills and capabilities to the platform

4. Ensuring the platform is the signal and not noise (insight into work/ skills demanded versus being a distraction to managers and talent)

5. Trust in the platform/system

The Role of AI and Algorithms: Taylorism on Steroids versus Democratized Work Empowerment

Much has been written about the power of AI in transforming work coordination and worker performance. Amazon has received patents for a wristband designed to guide the movements of warehouse workers with the use of vibrations to nudge them to be more efficient. IBM has applied for a patent for technology that can monitor its workforce with sensors that track pupil dilation and facial expressions and then use data on employees' sleep quality and meeting schedule to deploy drones that deliver a caffeinated liquid so employees can work without needing a coffee break.[4]

This might seem like the worst of Taylorism on steroids, an exploitive and intrusive approach to work. Certainly, there are many risks to consider, but AI is a critical enabling capability for realizing the full promise of the new work operating system. Using AI need not equate to exploiting workers. A term was coined for this in the CHREATE project, where teams of HR leaders envisioned the future of work and HR management: "democratized" work.[5] This term encompasses the idea of a more diverse and inclusive array of work arrangements and talent sources, as we have discussed earlier. However, it is also a play on the word "democracy" to capture the possibility that the new work operating system and its supporting technologies will disperse and make more transparent the information and decision frameworks that support the new operating system. Workers, leaders, policymakers, and others will be able to see a more complete picture at a more granular and deconstructed level. The result may be vastly increased empowerment for workers.

In chapter 1 we discussed how AI can rapidly deconstruct jobs and processes to identify the underlying tasks and activities. We also illustrated how it can be harnessed to continuously analyze work to determine the optimal combinations of humans and automation and the ideal type of human engagement option for a given task. In chapter 3 and chapter 4, we discussed AI-powered internal marketplaces that seamlessly match all the skills and capabilities of talent within an organization to the many different tasks and activities posted by managers. AI is fundamental to enabling the "many-to-many" matching between skills or capabilities and work in various shapes and guises. Absent the core AI, managers would be limited to their legacy role of matching an employee to a job.

Unilever provides an example of using AI to tap the positive value of the new work operating system while minimizing its more insidious side effects.

How Unilever Redefined Leadership in the New Work Operating System

Unilever illustrates this point through its objective to lead with purpose.[6] The company's previous CEO, Paul Polman, regarded sustainability not just as the right thing to do but as an essential component of growth. In 2010, Polman launched a "sustainable living development plan." Its goals included helping more than one billion people improve their hygiene and living conditions, reducing the impact of Unilever's operations on the environment, and promoting gender parity in its factories.

For Polman, the incentive is clear: businesses cannot thrive in a world in which people don't. Protect people and the environment, and you will protect the future of your enterprise. From reducing packaging to halving factory water waste and distributing free health and hygiene products to remote communities, Unilever no longer has a separate corporate social responsibility department; it is at the very heart of how it does its work. Current CEO Alan Jope and CHRO Leena Nair have continued and further accelerated this vision. The following case study from our work with Unilever details its Framework for the Future of Work.[7] It seamlessly connects an individual's purpose with the evolving nature of work and the need to ensure the continued relevance of the workforce. Unilever's strategy is "Purpose-Led, Future-Fit." The company aims to prove that purpose-led brands, businesses, and people deliver improved financial and societal impact by ensuring all their brands have a deeper and authentic societal and environmental purpose.

Unilever developed a work operating system anchored in the organization's responsibility to generate and sustain employability and its need to accelerate its own capabilities. It committed to meeting these with the Framework for the Future of Work that includes increased investment in lifelong learning and new forms of employment. The framework aims to provide Unilever employees with a purpose-driven future fit social contract of work that reflects perpetual change and to simultaneously enable business transformation that aligns with the organization's purpose:

1. **Ignite lifelong learning.** Unilever will proactively ensure all employees have a "My Future Fit Plan" and are deliberately building their future employability for new roles within or outside Unilever. Each employee must identify one or more future pathways for themselves among four different options: upskilling for the person's evolving role, reskilling for a different role within Unilever, reskilling for jobs

outside of Unilever, or transitioning to platform-based work within Unilever.

2. **Change with unions through collaboration, not confrontation.** Because 80 percent of Unilever's units are unionized, the framework risks strikes, negotiations, and protests that would undermine their purpose-led agenda. The company aims to work with employees and union representatives to build awareness, facilitate dialogue, and proactively cocreate employee plans. This collaboration with the unions ensures a partnership that is collectively vested in the continued relevance of the workforce for a changing world regardless of its tenure within Unilever. This is a very different relationship to the typical one between management and unions where management seeks to maximize flexibility and reduce costs while the union seeks to preserve employment and maximize rewards.

3. **Redefine the Unilever work system.** Unilever will develop new forms of employment within the organization, whereby employees have the option to move between fixed and flex employment. The company has already had great success with its Flex Experiences platform[8] that uses AI to quickly match people with project opportunities. It allows employees to work on projects for a small or large proportion of time, increase the depth of their current skills, or build new skills and experiences in a flexible way. The platform has come into its own as business agility became critical for business continuity during the COVID-19 pandemic. Unilever's marketing plans, supply chain, logistics, and product manufacture all needed to work at speed to respond to evolving consumer needs and expectations. This meant getting information and analytics out to the frontline to help teams respond to changes as the virus spread. For example, the company wanted to analyze internal data on sales, cash, and supply chain and compare them to the external factors such as infection rates and changing consumer behavior. To do so, the company turned to the Flex platform to build a COVID-19 information and analytics squad of talent with a diverse set of skills and experiences including data scientists, business analysts, project managers, and

user experience designers. Not only did the platform allow the company to address this challenge at speed with all the skills required, but it did so with all the efficiency and effectiveness that comes about when you can match the skills of a worker to the deconstructed work. Pilot schemes are also underway in the UK to "pool" people to share with other organizations. Figure 6.1 illustrates Unilever's Framework for the Future of Work.

Three features of the Unilever work operating system are particularly noteworthy. First, the new Unilever work system requires that workers shift from being told what training to undertake to instead charting their own development paths by using the new system to understand how their work will change and choosing when and how to respond. This can include upskilling for the current reinvented job, reskilling when their new job won't exist, preparing for emerging roles within or outside Unilever, and outskilling to embrace alternative working arrangements, with financial security partially provided by Unilever. It is important to note that Unilever does not merely provide reskilling for job openings that may exist elsewhere; the company leverages its network of relationships to support the employee's placement. The entire system is predicated on the deconstruction of jobs and skills so

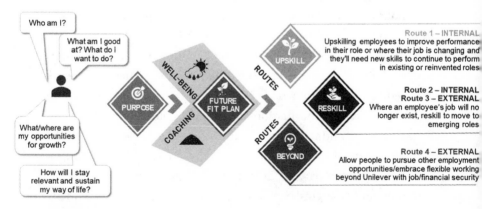

Figure 6.1
Unilever's Framework for the Future of Work

workers and the organization can shine a bright light on how various tasks are changing and the resulting implications for their skills.

Second, the new Unilever work system requires a fundamentally different leadership mindset and model. It requires leaders to operate in agile ways that transcend traditional organization structures and roles (e.g., by using the Flex Experiences platform to tackle an emerging challenge instead of attempting to hire employees into full-time jobs). We will discuss this in more detail below. It also requires enabling processes like compensation, budgeting, and performance measurement to be aligned and supportive of these new ways of working.

Third, the new work operating system starts with the individual, specifically their purpose and ambition. This then translates into an overall plan to ensuring their continued well-being and development and a future fit plan for ensuring their continued relevance. This leads to the four aforementioned potential options for each individual.

From Managing/Supervising Jobholders to Continual Work Crafting and Negotiation

Earlier in this book, we noted the term *job crafting*. Even the traditional work operating system with fixed jobs offers workers some discretion in their work tasks, relationships, and the meaning they attach to their work. Evidence suggests that job crafting allows workers to reduce work strain, increase work challenges, and thus increase their work engagement. These approaches are typically called job crafting, but in fact they have always relied on deconstructed job elements to understand and define the work content that jobholders craft and the process through which they craft it.

How might "good work" be defined as workers deconstruct and reconstruct their work to enhance its value and motivating potential? There is no single accepted definition, and of course the definition of good work will vary with the particular worker's characteristics and life situation, the organization's strategy, the nature of the work and its contribution, and so on. As one example, the Chartered Institute of Personnel and Development (CIPD), an HR professional association in the UK, identified these six dimensions as relevant to a job quality index for the UK:[9]

- pay and other rewards
- intrinsic characteristics of work (variety, autonomy, task identity, significance/purpose, knowledge of results, etc.)
- terms of engagement (type of contract, duration, security, etc.)
- health and safety
- work-life balance
- representation and voice

The new work operating system will increase work crafting because the deconstructed work elements become more fluid and more visible through vehicles such as internal and external talent marketplaces and automation-driven work redesign. Moreover, a lasting effect of COVID-19 and other disruptions is to empower workers to redesign their work. The result was often newly reconstructed work with greater productivity, personal growth, and well-being. That means that leaders, managers, and workers will be in continuing negotiation about work and work arrangements. Traditionally, such negotiations occurred between organizations and labor unions or other worker collectives. Under the old work operating system, such negotiations were infrequent and could assume stable jobs and job assignments. In contrast, in the new work operating system, this negotiation process will be more continual, more personalized, and more dispersed. Rather than relying on one group of negotiators who periodically meet to hash out a contract, the new work operating system will require managers and workers to negotiate in real time. That means organizations must equip frontline managers and workers with tools to accomplish these negotiations with the least amount of unnecessary contention and the maximum level of mutually beneficial outcomes.

There are many tools and frameworks for achieving such goals. For example, a perennial and well-supported framework is the "mutual gains" approach to bargaining. The elements are[10]

- preparation and estimating BATNA (yours and the other parties' "best alternative to a negotiated agreement"; understanding your own and the other parties' interests that go beyond their stated demands);

- value creation without commitment (the parties should declare a period of "inventing without committing," advancing "what if?" options to try to discover new interests and opportunities for joint gain);

- value distribution (define the criteria to determine how each party will justify that they received a "fair share" of the value created, and avoid bargaining from a single position); and

- follow through (imagine the future challenges and solutions and potential sources of conflict, ambiguity, and uncertainty; specify how to monitor delivery on commitments, resolve conflicts and confusion, align incentives with commitments, and help others who will implement the agreement).

Imagine if all managers and workers were equipped with such tools and were encouraged to use them to craft new solutions and arrangements as work is deconstructed and reconstructed. In the new work operating system, the success of management and leadership will often rest on the success of far larger and more dispersed negotiators. Broad one-size-fits-all policies and episodic formal contract negotiations will be less effective.

The success of the new work operating system will be significantly determined by the capabilities of the workers and managers as they negotiate real-time work deconstruction and reinvention.

Leadership Capabilities Shift from Hierarchy/Authority to Projects/Influence

Jonathan Donner was the vice president of global learning and capability development at Unilever, from 2009 to 2016, a strategic advisor and chief of the Capability Development Branch of the United Nations Food Programme, and director of executive development at Amazon. He now advises many organizations about the future of leadership and organizational capability. Donner and Boudreau described the following vision of leadership in the new work operating system in *Sloan Management Review*.[11]

The new work operating system will require a profound change in the mindset and behavior of leaders. It requires managers to think in terms of how tasks and projects are accomplished, not how jobs are organized. It will require leaders/managers to become skilled at orchestrating a broad array of different resources—some human, some not; some employees, some not—to execute those tasks. Moreover, as talent gains greater agency to choose the most desirable projects and project leaders, the relationship between managers and workers will become increasingly less hierarchical.

The new work operating system will require new leadership and manager capabilities that will vary depending on "levels" or roles. Organization-level leaders will (a) set the meta task or overall mission of the organization, (b) define and prioritize the required tasks, and (c) define the standards, goals conditions, supporting systems, and resources. This organization-level leadership will support leaders and managers throughout the organization, who will evolve toward *project leaders* who organize and optimize around tasks.

The new work operating system will lead to a culture and operating approach with a more overriding focus on task achievement, which drives strategic decisions and judgment about how best to combine humans and automation and assemble and flex those resources.

Of course, leadership has always meant creating conditions for organization members to achieve their best contribution, but the new work operating system fundamentally changes *how*. Here are some of the required capabilities and approaches for future leaders and managers in a system of work without jobs:

From digital savvy to technological fluency. In the new work operating system, deconstruction and reconstruction that combines humans and automation will require leaders to perpetually anticipate how technology and automation affect work. That means constantly balancing new innovations with viability and practicality and explaining new combinations of human and automated work to employees. Decisions about whether automation will replace, augment, or reinvent human work will need to be made continually at the task/project level—and will have to reflect an up-to-the-minute understanding of technological capabilities.

From process execution to project guidance. The organization will increasingly be a landscape of ongoing and evolving projects rather than a collection of defined and organized processes. Managers will constantly source talent within and beyond the traditional organization and rapidly assemble teams based on required skills and capabilities. Knowledge workers will increasingly connect with projects virtually through technology, so this evolved project management will more prominently reflect automation, distance collaboration, and influence. In traditional systems, such project management and coordination might be accomplished by aligning to Gantt charts, for example, but the new system will require more real-time and perpetual coordination. Managers will continually apply tools much like those now used by Agile teams (scrums, sprints, hacks, etc.).

From hierarchical authority to empowerment and alignment. Hierarchical authority will be inadequate in the new system of work without jobs because workers will not be as tied to traditional reporting structures and project-based work requires teams to increasingly self-manage. The transparency of the new system will make work opportunities more visible through a continually updated array of options available to workers. Employees will demand more work that meets their personal preferences and seek the freedom to shift from project to project. Leaders will need to set strong frameworks that balance worker empowerment with accountability and consistency that reflects the broader task/mission. They will have to discern when and how to negotiate, whether to negotiate formally and informally, and how to attain team and individual alignment about how value will be created and shared.

From technical to humanistic work automation. Work automation increasingly requires work without jobs because optimal solutions are often visible only at the task and skill level. We will have more frequent, and visible, choices to make between replacing, augmenting, and reinventing the human worker[12]—in the last case by using technology to give humans entirely new and more valuable capabilities, which are only possible through automation. Such decisions will no longer be episodic, discussed in the context of a new robot or AI system, but rather will be a perpetual series of decisions by leaders and their teams. One issue that will gain prominence is potential bias when choosing whether tasks are done by human workers versus machines/automation. Leaders may assume that automation always produces greater predictability and efficiency. But as such choices will increasingly occur at the project level, managers will need a more nuanced understanding of what humans can contribute to aesthetic creativity, cultural perspective, and innovative potential.

From episodic to continual focus on diversity, equity, and inclusion. The traditional job-based system inclines leaders to consider diversity, equity, and inclusion (DEI) episodically, typically when hiring or considering promotions. As important as these events can be, it is the ongoing relationships and interactions that more often determine DEI success. A system of work without jobs puts the focus squarely on these ongoing interactions and presents far more frequent opportunities to choose, assign, reward, and develop team members as tasks/projects and team memberships are fluid and perpetually reinvented. This could significantly enhance DEI efforts by offering more opportunities for new work experiences than traditional job-based systems afford. Yet if bias persists, that same accelerated frequency can result in more noninclusive choices. Organizational leaders will need to create new processes for continually assessing whether work, and its remuneration, are distributed equitably.

The Foundational Pillar: Purpose-Led Work

In sum, the success of a system of work without jobs will rest increasingly on leaders and managers who consistently lead themselves and others with purpose. The essence of this change is distilled into a question posed by Rob Goffee and the late Gareth Jones: "Why should anyone be led by you?"[13] This question becomes even more important as human talent gains agency and autonomy to choose work from platforms in service of serial teams and multiple leaders.

Real-time leadership and management in a system of continually reinvented work means rethinking fundamentals such as attracting, retaining, motivating, and engaging workers. Talent will choose projects based on not only the desirability of the task (what will I do?) but also the "brand" of the leader (how will I be led?). To continually and successfully assemble teams in the new work operating system, leaders must nurture their now more transparent leadership brand and track record. We see this already as organizations track and codify leader/manager quality on internal talent marketplaces. Employees have ready access to a leader's leadership brand across projects on the platform. This brand will be revealed in the shadow leaders leave from their past projects and increasingly embodied in marketplace ratings by former team members on questions like "how much can you learn by working with them?" and "how open and flexible are they to innovation and different styles of work and contribution?" In the traditional job-based system, such questions are answered only obscurely and indirectly. The new system may embody something like a perpetually updated leader net promoter score (NPS), calculated as the percentage of promoters minus detractors based on the question "how likely are you to recommend us to a friend or colleague?" Today, NPS is a common tool to assess customer satisfaction, so the new work operating system could easily adapt the tool for leaders. The new system will make it acutely obvious how they are seen by followers who perpetually engage and reengage, much like customers who have repeated service or product experiences.

With leaders' reputations continually earned and confirmed via their track record of projects, they will have dramatically less lead time to effectively and inspirationally convey who they are and what guides them. As workers travel a career path of fast-changing tasks/project and roles, working serially for new project managers, they will increasingly discern which leaders share their higher aspirations for value beyond task success. The increased speed and granularity of work without jobs will prize leaders whose purpose is like the keel of a sailboat, steadying and guiding it toward a destination even as it tacks through shifting winds. Leaders who convey such sustainable purpose will be the ones best able to attract necessary talent.

Conclusion

The new work operating system of work without jobs and jobholders offers fundamental opportunities and challenges for future leaders and managers of all types. Will the jobs of CEOs, C-suite executives, and leaders/managers also be deconstructed and reconstructed? Yes, eventually, but we will leave this question for a future book. The more immediate question is, How will the new world of work alter management's responsibilities and priorities?

On the face of it, much remains the same: C-suite leaders will still set the strategic mission of the organization and define standards, goals, conditions, and resources. This will in turn support functional leaders, who establish systems to align and support midlevel leaders, who prioritize and translate organizational goals into strategic objectives for their unit. And frontline managers will continue to define and prioritize the processes and tasks required to meet these objectives.

All of these managers will have additional vital roles in the new work operating system. One role will be to set the standards and boundaries of the new work operating system, particularly when organizations are at the early stages of the transition. Not all work is best done in a deconstructed way, and the speed with which organizations adopt an approach of deconstructing jobs will vary based on their mission, strategy, processes, culture, and technology, among other factors.

The second vital role for high-level functional leaders will be to set the broad guardrails that define how work is both delineated and coordinated across functions. Functions such as finance, operations, facilities, legal, medical, HR, and IT will each establish certain boundaries and principles about how work is accomplished, coordinated, and shared. Currently, those guardrails are generally set when individuals take a job: for example, they are assigned access to certain IT systems, clearances to handle sensitive materials, or even the rights to enter facilities that require health and safety training. But as jobs are deconstructed into sets of capabilities or tasks, which could potentially be done by a wider variety of people including nonemployees, setting and adapting these guardrails will have to be done quickly and continually—and require rapid cross-functional coordination. New ways of organizing and assigning work will demand that the high-level leaders of the organization give increased attention to the work and how it is accomplished and shared. Underlying this must be an accepted model for how power and accountability are distributed— that must also evolve in step with how the organization adopts tools like internal talent marketplaces. This is the key to avoiding chaos and to ensuring that the new work operating system remains consistent with the broader strategy, purpose, and culture that defines the organization.

Meanwhile, frontline leaders will still organize and optimize the goals of their units and attend to the needs and desires of their workers but now in the currency of tasks and projects and worker skills and capabilities. They will evolve into project leaders who perpetually deconstruct projects into tasks and assemble workers into teams to accomplish those tasks based on their deconstructed capabilities. In many cases, workers will no longer be exclusively assigned to a leader through a stable job and hierarchy. In organizations that adopt "work without jobs" fully, the work and workers will be more free floating, and leaders and managers will quickly assemble and disassemble teams to achieve the broader unit and organizational goals.

All of this will mean that there are fewer places for leaders to hide and more opportunities to be seen. Leaders and managers will be defined less by title and credentials and more by achievements and character: what have they done and/or are capable of doing, and how have they done it? As we consider the new operating system further, it calls for strengthening and adapting some traditional leadership skills and building some new ones.

Upon first encounter, the new work operating system can seem to diminish the human dimension. However, work without jobs will actually *enhance* the impact of leaders' humanity, differentiating good from great organizations. Organizations that thrive will rely more on leaders/ managers who are capable of assembling, selecting, assessing, developing, motivating, and articulating purpose and alignment for short-term teams, formed by deconstructing and reconstructing work and workers. This new *agile, serial leadership* will require leaders/managers to excel at human leadership as they perpetually reinvent work; construct more transient, deconstructed, and highly efficient teams; and blend humans with technology.[14]

A Checklist for Getting Started

1. Have you identified your best opportunities to experiment with agile innovative work design?
2. Have you applied your existing agile innovation tools and processes to work design, using deconstructed work elements?
3. Have you considered where the work in your organization might be redesigned to exploit the coordination approaches of consulting firms?
4. Have you created systems to better understand how your workers are already *crafting* their jobs and how to tap into those activities through *work crafting*?
5. Have you provided your managers and workers with tools for mutual gains negotiation when it comes to work crafting about work deconstruction and reinvention?
6. Have you begun to equip your leaders and managers with the tools, competencies, and values needed to evolve to *project leaders* from traditional *job leaders*?

7 The New Work Operating System beyond the Organization

Previous chapters have shown you *how* to create and use a new work operating system that relies on deconstruction and reinvention. In this chapter we take up the question of *what social policies might be required to enable* the new work operating system in organizations. In particular, we consider social, public, and external stakeholder policies and issues. Of course, not only are such policies potentially valuable in implementing the new work operating system, but a new work operating system is also necessary to facilitate such policies.

Recall that the future of work is unevenly distributed.[1] Of course, much work, perhaps even the majority of the work for a few years, will still be adequately organized, governed, and regulated as traditional regular full-time jobs held by traditional employees. It will be governed under the umbrella and framework of employment and under the assumption that the employment relationship is sufficient to capture necessary relationships and transactions between those who provide work and those who need work done. Ultimately, however, an increasing portion of work will exist as deconstructed tasks, and an increasing portion of workers will interact with the workplace by being free to apply their deconstructed capabilities (e.g., skills, abilities, knowledge) in more fluid ways, liberated from the requirement that they try to fit themselves into a particular job.

This chapter will illustrate how deconstruction is central to implementing many of the social policy recommendations designed to make the work relationship more seamless, efficient, equitable, and transparent. Even regular full-time employment will increasingly take on the characteristics of this new work operating system, with efforts to meet these goals. Reformulating the fundamental unit of work from being a job and the worker as a jobholder (employee or contractor) offers insights and options that the traditional job-based system simply cannot accommodate.

From Employment, Jobs, and Jobholders toward Platforms

Recall from the introduction that virtually all social systems are still based on the concept of work as a job and worker as an employee. Citizens often demand that corporations, governments, and society address the hardship of work displacement, yet promises to preserve or repatriate the good jobs of the past are increasingly unrealistic. Frequently, the reference to "good jobs of the past" means preserving the same jobs that existed before but under very different economic conditions. For example, it is unrealistic to promise to preserve traditional jobs in coal mining when market and environmental forces are making coal mining not viable. The COVID-19 pandemic produced massive layoffs and vastly accelerated work restructuring. Traditional calls to retrain and redeploy laid-off workers into good jobs in high-demand industries were also joined by suggestions that workers' newfound desire for flexibility in work location and timing might be better served through rethinking on-demand work, organized as tasks on platforms.[2]

Such vital social issues demand solutions beyond jobs, including better platforms and better systems to support the discovery, usability, and awareness of these platforms. Just as the job and jobholder concepts are insufficient to meet the market-matching needs of the changing work ecosystem, they similarly are insufficient to meet essential human needs, such as income, healthcare, collective voice, healthcare security, and retirement funds. These additional needs might be better and more efficiently attached to platform work that exists as deconstructed work tasks and worker capabilities. Or they might be detached from work altogether in the form of a social safety net that does not depend on employment in jobs and thus would empower even greater experimentation with the new work operating system we have described. The World Economic Forum Charter of Principles for Good Platform Work shows how this well-respected global advocacy organization has begun to focus on platform work. The language offers a useful example of the sort of ideas policymakers may adopt in the future.

World Economic Forum Charter of Principles for Good Platform Work

1. Diversity and inclusion: Platforms should strive to be inclusive and usable by a diverse population of workers, and should encourage qualified participants from all national, religious, gender, sexual orientation and ethnic backgrounds, including persons with disabilities.

2. Safety and well-being: Platforms should have policies or guidelines in place, appropriate to the locations and modes of work, to help protect workers from health and safety risks, and should endeavor to protect and promote the physical and mental well-being of workers. Users/clients should acknowledge and adhere to the policies and guidelines.

3. Flexibility and fair conditions: Terms and conditions should be transparent, clearly stated, easily understandable, and provided to workers in an accessible form. Grounds and procedures for account deactivation should be clear, and platforms should work to establish processes to challenge decisions where relevant, with multi-stakeholder support if applicable. Processes should respect confidentiality where appropriate. Platforms should promote a culture of transparency and human accountability across use of algorithms, and ensure that fairness and non-discrimination are a priority in the design of algorithms.

4. Reasonable pay and fees: Workers should have full transparency on the basis for what they will earn before deciding whether to accept tasks. Where minimum wage thresholds exist, workers classified as employees should earn at least the minimum wage of their jurisdiction, proportional to the time spent actively working and accounting for reasonable expenses for their mode of work. Workers who set their own rates should be able to do so in a way that reflects market dynamics.

(continued)

(continued)

5. Social protection: Governments and platforms should collaborate to ensure that workers have access to a comprehensive set of reliable and affordable social protections and benefits that meet their individual needs, taking into account local conditions, and are well informed about their options. This process should take into account workers' views and feedback on their needs. Regulation should be adapted as appropriate to enable platforms to support the provision of such benefits to workers who are not classified as employees.

6. Learning and development: Platform work should encourage and enable individual professional development. All stakeholders—notably governments and platforms—should collaborate to ensure that workers have access to affordable educational and upskilling programmes to support their professional development.

7. Voice and participation: Workers should be able to express their views on platform guidelines and practices to the platform, and platforms should provide processes, channels and/or forums as appropriate for those discussions to occur. Platforms should ensure that workers have access to transparent and accountable mechanisms, where applicable, for resolving disputes with users/clients and with other workers within a reasonable timeframe.

8. Data management: Workers should be able to view a complete history of their platform use and, where applicable, an aggregate review rating at any time, in an easy-to-read, understandable and transferable format, in accordance with jurisdictional requirements and based on the development of appropriate formats for transferability.

Adapted from "Charter of Principles for Good Platform Work," World Economic Forum, 2018, http://www3.weforum.org/docs/WEF_Charter_of_Principles_for_Good_Platform _Work.pdf.

Work Platform Social, Policy, and Organization Challenges

The promises of a platform approach to work, built upon an operating system of work deconstruction, are significant, including social benefits such as bringing marginalized or poorer workers into the mainstream of the work market. Deconstructing work tasks and looking beyond the traditional idea of a job can be keys to work flexibility, geographic diversity, expanding demand in untapped populations, expanded income, improved matching, more formalized and transparent work transactions, and more reliable work payment systems.

While the new operating system of deconstructed work can operate within and alongside traditional employment, many of its benefits and challenges are best understood through the lens of platform work, so it is enlightening to consider how social policy limits and might advance the experience of platform workers.

The World Economic Forum, having constructed the charter shown in the sidebar, also noted these remaining and formidable global challenges of platform work:[3]

Benefits and social protections. Platform workers are often classified as independent contractors, which means they do not have the same safety net as salaried employees and associated rights and benefits such as holidays, sick pay, unemployment insurance, and pensions. Platforms are often limited in their ability to offer such protections by regulatory constraints that only provide for such benefits in the traditional employment context.

Reasonable pay. A key challenge for some lower-skilled work is to ensure that incomes are high enough to support a reasonable quality of life. Because platform workers are often classified as independent contractors, they are often not covered by minimum pay laws.

Dignity and interest. Platform work may commoditize certain tasks within jobs, leading to uniformly mundane and repetitive work.

Security. There is a need to ensure an appropriate balance of risk with regards to the availability of work shared across the consumer, platform, and worker. For example, in a traditional employment relationship, the risk of periods of low demand is borne by the employer; if demand is low, the worker is still paid (in the short to medium term). In the platform economy, the risk is carried primarily by the worker— even more so as workers typically lack access to safety nets. Workers also often lack protection against removal from a platform.

Upskilling. Workers may lack opportunities to reskill, upskill, and access training opportunities through their work. This is particularly important in the context of the fourth industrial revolution, where rapid technological change means ongoing reskilling and upskilling are increasingly important to ensure continued employability.

Representation. Platform workers often do not benefit from the traditional instruments available in many societies to ensure workers' voices are heard and matter and that their rights are respected, such as collective bargaining and representation.

Balance of power. While a successful work/service platform needs strong network effects, excessive market concentration can be detrimental for worker conditions.

Next, we describe several broader global policy and social challenges that are often cited as pivotal to a more fluid work ecosystem, which will be necessary in advancing the new work operating system of deconstructed work and workers. For each social challenge, we note the significance of deconstructed work. As we noted above, it is enlightening to consider how social policy currently limits the experience of platform workers, and how it might be updated to advance such experience.

Work "Culture" and "Engagement" beyond Traditional Employment

Can nontraditional workers actually be *more* engaged and satisfied than traditional employees? Wayne Cascio and John Boudreau conducted a review of scholarly studies.[4] The following paragraph provides just a few examples of key studies about worker attitudes and motivation, comparing freelance or contingent workers to regular full-time workers.

A meta-analysis of seventy-two studies involving over 230,000 workers found, on average, contingent workers experience slightly lower job satisfaction than permanent employees but that it varies by the type of contingent work.[5] Some contingent workers (e.g., agency workers) experience lower job satisfaction, while other contingent workers (e.g., contractors) do not. A survey of temporary workers in Europe found that prior experience as a temporary worker was not associated with job insecurity, job satisfaction, or organizational commitment, but job insecurity increased closer to the end of temporary contracts.[6] A study across a large a national sample of Australian temporary workers found that compared to permanent workers, temporary agency workers are less satisfied with job security and hours worked but are equally satisfied with their pay.[7] In another study, researchers compared permanent and contingent workers doing the same work in six US locations of a telecommunications company and found contingent workers perceived their work as *more motivating* due to higher "task identity" (a complete and visible work outcome) and knowledge of results despite perceiving less job security.[8] Contingent workers also had higher "growth need strength" (need for personal accomplishment, learning, and development).

Though the findings are mixed, patterns are emerging that suggest how leaders can increase engagement among contingent workers:

- Workers engaged through temporary staff firms or direct hire arrangements prefer permanent employment, while independent contractors prefer nonpermanent arrangements.

- Those who voluntarily choose or prefer contingent work have more positive experiences than those who chose it for lack of alternatives.

- Emotional support from coworkers and supervisors is positively related to contingent worker commitment. This is true of commitment both to the temporary firm that placed the workers and the organization where they deliver their work. Support from the client organization has been found to "spill over" into commitment to the temporary organization placing workers with that client.

- Workers who perceive their "psychological contract" with an organization as social and emotional (versus merely transactional and economic) tend to be more willing to go the extra mile by working longer, helping others, and supporting change. When temporary workers have a lasting relationship with the organization with the possibility of renewing their temporary contract or converting from temporary to permanent, they develop a similar psychological contract to permanent workers.

- Even beyond the psychological contract, expectations of continuity positively associate with temporary worker attitudes and performance. One study found that temporary agency workers who have opportunities to transition to standard employment arrangements have more positive attitudes toward supervisors and coworkers and perform better than their peers in *permanent* work arrangements.[9]

Thus, it seems quite plausible that work systems based on the new operating model of deconstructed work, combined with platform-based work systems, may, with appropriate design, be capable of achieving high levels of engagement and commitment and that work culture is not necessarily limited to a traditional employment relationship.

We already see how platform workers and their ecosystem provide community, psychological contracts, culture, and self-regulating market mechanisms. One example is Upwork, one of the world's largest freelance platforms. Stephane Kasriel, the former CEO of Upwork, observed that the Upwork community is like a sports league: while all players are strong, simply putting a random subset of them together for the first time (which is what tends to happen frequently) doesn't lead to a high-performing team.[10] He mused that perhaps Upwork should instead encourage reusing the same subset multiple times on different projects so they get better at working together and, ultimately, deliver better work to their clients.

Kasriel also noted that enterprises that are clients of Upwork build pools of freelancers. One feature of the Upwork platform is that it enables clients to build microscopic versions of the overall marketplace. So instead of choosing freelancers from among the entire pool of over twelve million workers, enterprise managers choose among a few dozen or a few hundred. Those freelancers do repeat engagements with the client, learn more intimately how to make the client happy, and then get better ratings over time.

Kasriel observed that just as organizational context is critical for knowledge workers as employees, context is equally important when the worker is a freelancer. The best Upwork clients help freelancers learn about their company's needs. In part, that means familiarizing and connecting freelancers to the social network by informing them about the relevant stakeholders, their preferences, and so on. Most clients are not very good at optimizing the right amount of access and context to their freelancers, so the freelancers don't get the best results, end up less satisfied with the relationship, and are less likely to work with the client again.

Platform Workers as a Social Network[11]

The potential for the new work operating system to redefine the concept of organizations, and their relationships to the external system of workers, society, and economies, is vividly illustrated if you consider the organization as a social network. For decades, research has used organizational network analysis (ONA) to measure the level and nature of interactions between individuals.[12] Such measures then allow mathematical analysis that can produce the now-familiar social network map, which shows individuals as nodes and connections between them as lines. Such maps have been proven useful in identifying the clusters of individuals who interact frequently and comprise naturally occurring teams, the value of "boundary-spanning" individuals who create links between otherwise-isolated clusters, the hidden social "influencers" who may not be visible in the traditional hierarchy, and the value of "weak ties" that can allow information to flow more freely than through "strong ties" that may inhibit frank interchanges.

Research by Rob Cross and his associates found that 3–5 percent of the people usually account for 20–35 percent of the value-added collaborations in most organizations.[13] Yet even in the most sophisticated enterprises, and even when applying ONA to their employees, organizations tend to miss about half of these central players. In the new work operating system, the "network" becomes even more important, as the individual workers are no longer so easily categorized as jobholders and their interactions with others may be based more on their deconstructed skills, capabilities, or relationships than on their job." Such networks will often include workers outside the traditional organization, who have been engaged as platform workers, freelancers, contractors, and so on. Most organizations seldom apply ONA to include workers outside the traditional employment relationship.

Organizations are experimenting with new systems that provide greater visibility to your entire workforce, including employees, contractors, temporary workers, freelancers, and even volunteers. Yet even these systems typically track only headcount, skills, and project assignments. That's like managing regular employees only with traditional organization charts. Just as ONA can offer insights regarding employees, it can also offer insights about nonemployees. Implications include the following:

- Rewards for freelancers and contractors are typically set only based on their skill levels, individual project performance, and customer ratings, yet their network quality likely affects their performance similarly to regular employees. Research shows that for employees, it is not the size of the network but the quality and mutuality of the connections[14] that leads to performance. If the same is true for the extended workforce, then organizations should measure the network quality and position of freelancers, contractors, and others.

- Just as ONA can reveal employees who are too peripheral (representing untapped skills and resources) and those who are too central (representing potential victims of collaborative overload and burnout), the same could be measured for nonemployees. This could help identify untapped resources that can be harnessed by including them more fully in the employer's network or candidates that are so overloaded that they are unlikely to perform well—even if their past projects were highly rated.

- ONA research[15] shows that newcomers are more successful if they create "pull" that makes them sought-after rather than trying to create "push" through aggressive personal selling. Organizations can use this finding to encourage and support nonemployee workers in making themselves visible and desirable to key network members among the organization's employees. Just as ONA suggests that employees who stay beyond two to three years must shift their networks to become broader and deeper, perhaps nonemployee workers who have had several "tours of duty" with the organization should also be encouraged to connect to projects beyond their initial network.

A Global "Rosetta Stone of Work"

One fundamental requirement to enable a more fluid work ecosystem is that worker capabilities and work requirements are transparently and easily identified and matched. The matching task becomes exponentially more complex when the work is deconstructed. What is needed is a common language for the deconstructed work and worker elements, a language that represents a standard that is then adopted by workers and work organizations. The ultimate need is for a universal translation and matching platform or system. John Boudreau suggested the term "Rosetta Stone of work."[16]

When such capabilities are embedded in jobs and jobholders, such identification and matching is typically embedded in an HR system that tracks the demands of jobs and the capabilities of employees and applicants who match those job requirements. Work demands are tracked as job requisitions and are filled with internal employees or external applicants who are fully qualified or very close to qualified to do the entire set of tasks included in the job.

As we have seen, a more fluid and deconstructed work ecosystem demands that the work requirements be represented as tasks and the worker as capabilities. This has an immediate advantage in that it will naturally identify workers who might be less than 100 percent qualified for a typical job but are qualified enough to take on the necessary tasks, when those tasks are freed from the job. It also identifies workers who are "adjacently" qualified, perhaps possessing 80 percent of the needed capabilities for the job, with the other 20 percent of the needed qualifications being easily developed through online training, community college courses, organizational training, or on-the-job learning. Increasing the recruitment net to include such workers might vastly increase the pool of available workers, compared to waiting for a candidate who is willing to join the organization as an employee and possesses 100 percent of the qualifications.

As we noted in chapter 4, representing the work as tasks and the worker as capabilities demands a far more granular translation and matching system than when matching an entire worker with an entire job. It is even difficult to compare intact jobs. Recall the example from chapter 4, where even within the military, the job of yeoman differs across the branches. Even a relatively comparable job such a "retail associate" might encompass very different tasks across different retailers, and so a national or global system that can track deconstructed work tasks and worker skills/capabilities will involve exponentially greater complexity than any system that exists today.

We envision a platform that will resemble Amazon-Netflix-Google, where the work transactions themselves inform an automated set of AI translators and optimization algorithms to fashion an ontology that not only includes qualifications but also tracks "adjacencies" and "development paths" that span organizations, tours of duty, projects, badges, and so on. Is this farfetched? One might have said the same thing about the exponential complexity of a system that would deconstruct products into their features and customers into their desires, across products as varied as books and fresh produce. Amazon proved the practicality and market value of tackling that complexity. Google already has online translation and search engines that will show available jobs suitable for an infantry commander (such as distribution center manager, operations manager, training manager); one simply types the phrase "jobs for veterans" into the Google Search engine. Such tools are likely just the beginning. Understanding the new work operating system offers a way to anticipate this future.

Tools or taxonomies like these have immensely important implications for policymakers, regulators, governments, organizational leaders, worker collectives, and others concerned with a more fluid, equitable, and efficient work system. Who will "own" the data in such a system?

Will the burgeoning market to build such platforms eventually resolve into single-company players (such as Google or Amazon)? Or will the global community invest in open-source systems that will be available to work providers and work seekers globally?

Universal Health Coverage

The World Economic Forum defines universal health coverage (UHC) as "ensuring all individuals and communities have access to the healthcare they need." UHC does not mean healthcare is free but that personal out-of-pocket payments do not deter people from using health services and people are protected from "catastrophic health expenditure" (i.e., spending more than 30 percent of their household income on health)."[17] It notes that by 2030, that gap in financing UHC in the fifty-four poorest countries will be about $176 billion per year, 20–40 percent of health spending will be wasted, and people in developing countries will spend half a trillion dollars each year on out-of-pocket health expenses, pushing one hundred million people globally into poverty.

How can nations reduce waste and improve health care and labor mobility? The World Bank Group suggested four priority areas.[18] First, it is important to ramp up investments in affordable, quality primary healthcare. Health systems based on a foundation of strong primary healthcare are more efficient and equitable, producing higher value and better health outcomes: more resources to detect and treat conditions early, before they become more serious, will not only save lives but also reduce health costs. Second, it is important to engage the private sector and unlock new models for health financing and delivery. Third, we must go beyond health to improve health outcomes and support communities by improving education, broadening social services, and creating jobs. Fourth, we need to change the way health is financed so countries get better outcomes for the money they are spending.

With regard to platform workers, the World Economic Forum further notes that "even when platform workers have statutory eligibility to benefits, they may not be able to access them in practice."[19] Up to 70 percent of platform workers in EU economies reported being unable to access schemes such as childcare and housing benefits.[20] This may be due in part because workers are limited in their ability to transfer benefits when moving between platforms. A further issue may be that independent workers, as small businesses, receive less favorable pricing on healthcare than large companies.

The benefits and costs of UHC are complex, and institutional and tradition barriers exist, particularly in countries with well-entrenched systems that tie health benefits to regular traditional employment. However, UHC has proven cost-effective and successful, both in advanced Western economies and notably in poorer countries and societies. One analysis of developing-country experience with UHC concluded that "the message that striking rewards can be reaped from serious attempts at instituting—or even moving toward—universal healthcare is hard to miss. The critical ingredients of success that have emerged from these studies appear to include a firm political commitment to providing universal healthcare, running workable elementary healthcare and preventive services covering as much of the population as possible, paying serious attention to good administration in healthcare and ancillary public services and arranging effective school education for all. Perhaps most importantly, it means involving women in the delivery of health and education in a much larger way than is usual in the developing world."[21] Even in the United States, with its tradition of tying health coverage to employment, innovations have arisen to offer health benefits for platform and "gig" workers. Stride Health offers an app to help such workers search for and enroll in health plans. The Affordable Care Act, while politically controversial, is another attempt to offer health coverage to a broader spectrum of US workers and residents and close the gap to UHC.

As the new work operating system of deconstructed work and workers extends to an increasing amount of the work domain, the benefits of UHC become even more apparent and essential for future workers.

Universal Basic Income and Microfinancing

The notion of a universal basic income (UBI) has enjoyed attention for decades. It is a government program that delivers a periodic payment to all or certain individuals in a population, and it does not require work and is not means tested.[22] A different, but related, idea is a "guaranteed basic income" (GBI), in which a level of income is established, and then individuals whose income falls below that level are given subsidies that bring their income up to that minimum level.

The idea is not without controversy but gained attention as the accelerating effects of work automation became apparent, with one US presidential hopeful, Andrew Yang, making the idea a key part of his presidential platform. He suggested that technology might allow workers to stop doing the most dangerous, repetitive, and boring jobs. However, if this meant that Americans had no source of income—no ability to pay for groceries, buy homes, save for education, or start families with confidence—then this promising future could be very dark. He suggested that the labor participation rate, at only 62.7 percent in 2019, may get much worse as self-driving cars and other technologies come online. Yang proposed a Freedom Dividend—funded by a value-added tax—that would allow more Americans to benefit from automation. The Freedom Dividend would provide money to cover the basic income while enabling workers to look for a better job, start a business, go back to school, take care of loved ones, or work toward their next opportunity.[23]

The vast economic depression brought on by the COVID-19 crisis that began in 2020 produced an unprecedented level of fiscal relief across a wide spectrum of countries. That relief often took on the characteristics of UBI/GBI by offering employers funding to cover their payroll expenses if they kept their workers employed during the downturn or by providing supplemental unemployment benefits that offered enhanced payments to raise the income levels of laid-off employees. In the wake of the COVID-19 crisis, greater attention was paid to the potential for programs like UBI/GBI. A University of London research professor, writing for the World Economic Forum, suggested that such systems should (1) not be lump-sum payments, (2) be designed so that everyone has "equal command over subsistence resources" (those with disabilities or frailties would receive more), (3) not be means tested (to avoid poorer individuals facing the trap of giving up benefits to take work), and be (4) guaranteed and nonwithdrawable for a set period of time or until a measurable economic recovery level.[24]

With the COVID-19 pandemic and its associated effect on employees, much of this debate shifted to the effect of such policies on regular full-time workers who were displaced from their traditional jobs. However, the policy had also received prior attention from those addressing the gig economy or platform workers. A blog from the University of Oxford's iLabor project in 2017 suggested that a typical policy response tends to be to regulate gig work back into the mold of standard employment.[25] In contrast, basic income takes a different angle by providing workers with a level of security and predictability over their income that is independent of work. Plus, by providing workers with a fallback option, a sufficiently high basic income empowers them to turn down bad gigs. So rather than *regulating* employer-employee relations, basic income allows them to negotiate terms on a more level playing field.

As workers operate in a more deconstructed and fluid ecosystem, their work may increasingly fall outside of the traditional employment relationship. They may begin to take on the characteristics of what the World Bank has called "informal workers," who run very small businesses or work as paid service workers (e.g., domestic workers, household cleaners). In this regard, they would fall between "formal workers" who have traditional employment contracts that may provide some income or other protections and those who are not working and can access some social programs to provide subsistence income or other assistance.

Similarly, there is a vast untapped worker population in lower-income countries. The new work operating system and deconstructed platform work holds the promise of engaging that workforce more fully. We commonly encounter platform workers from lower-income countries who have amassed a client portfolio that includes some of the largest companies in the world or some of the top entertainment producers. They often credit the platform for offering them the vehicle to become known and to demonstrate their capabilities.

Thus, it is instructive to see what the World Bank recommended in 2020 as a response to COVID-19 for informal workers. The task of building up and accessing the workers in lower-income countries requires leaders and policymakers to rethink many of the traditional ways of financing such workers. The World Bank noted that in lower-income countries where informality is high, policy instruments targeted to protect private sector firms reach only a small portion of the workers in the economy. Availability of finance for smaller firms and their workers should be a priority since such firms and workers are not efficiently reached through formal instruments such as taxation policies or wage subsidies. It noted that this support can be triaged by commercial banks, microfinance institutions, digital lending platforms, corporate supply chains, local governments, communities, or other intermediaries. However, for them to participate, there must be accountability measures and incentives such as portfolio risk-sharing and guarantees for the intermediaries against potential losses. The World Bank also noted that the distinction between micro firms and individuals is blurred, so the support must take the form of cash transfers directly to informal workers rather than to informal firms.[26]

Several major US cities began experimenting with UBI in 2021, including Pittsburgh (Pennsylvania), Compton (California), Columbia (South Carolina), and Jackson (Mississippi). It has been particularly fascinating to see how nuanced many of these experiments are, targeting specific circumstances or issues versus the traditional approach of more generally targeting those living in poverty. Specifically, some of the other factors motivating these experiments included pursuing racial justice and addressing family needs. Regardless of the specific goal, all of these experiments would be more feasible if they were built upon a new work system that is more deconstructed and not limited by an exclusive focus on traditional employment arrangements.[27]

In sum, while much remains unknown about the actual effects of UBI/GBI and enhanced access to financing for platform workers and small businesses, the aftermath of economic shocks such as COVID-19, which also revealed the precarious position of many underserved populations, seems likely to keep the idea prominent. As work becomes increasingly deconstructed, this prominence should accelerate the consideration of how best to orient such programs to allow workers greater discretion and fluidity to construct work based on its deconstructed components to best match their deconstructed capabilities and development desires.

Unions, Collectives, Social, and Worker Voice on Platforms

What is the future of labor unions? The question of unions and worker collectives extends to work platforms. In 2015, Seattle was required to select a union to represent Uber drivers.[28] The U.S. Chamber of Commerce opposed the law, saying it would "inhibit the free flow of commerce,"[29] and a US appeals court revived that challenge.[30]

A paper from the European Trade Union Institute (ETUI) mapped Western European examples of collective representation of platform workers.[31] It noted that unions of traditional trades were the model until the beginning of the twentieth century. The model was then overshadowed, though not totally replaced, by industrial unionism, peaking in the 1960s to the 1970s. The ETUI proposed that a new model is emerging, one that features multisectoral or general unions encompassing industry and services.

Platform work arrangements, where work consists of deconstructed tasks, often done as piecework, can present exploitive possibilities due to blurred boundaries between worker private and work life, inadequate compensation for worker capital investments, little health and safety monitoring, vague surveillance practices, and so on. Because few countries have well-developed regulatory practices, the "institutional power" of workers (rights to unionize and collectively bargain) do not exist. Platform workers' "structural" bargaining power may replace institutional power. Structural bargaining power increases when workers possess unique skills and the ability to disrupt production processes by withholding their work. In addition, even today when most platform workers are only loosely committed to platform work (such as when it is a source of supplemental income in addition to a more traditional full-time job), the social media aspects of such work often amplify the voices of a small number of activists. They can rally platform workers by identifying issues seen as potentially unjust, making such platform work more attractive to a larger number of workers in the new work operating system. One example is in the ETUI paper, where it described the collective action of bike-riding food couriers across Western Europe in 2017 and 2018, who collectively "logged out" of the platform in protest to a shift from pay by the hour to pay by the delivery. The paper noted that platforms offer several unique collective voice amplification features:[32]

- mass self-communication networks that can span regions, countries, or even the globe

- breeding grounds for self-organized associations that boost associational power and even offer alliances with traditional trade unions that can provide expertise, organizing power, and funding (the largest German union, IG Metall, opened membership to platform workers in 2016)

- social media access to public opinion that can produce consumer or regulatory pressure for reforms

We have shown in this book that an increasing amount of work will become platform work or even regular full-time employment will increasingly resemble platform work. It is thus vital that leaders, workers, and policymakers learn lessons from today's platforms about representation and "voice" that go beyond the traditional employment and union relationship of the old work operating system.

In the new work operating system, unions may offer advantages. Organizations often resist unionization to maintain strategic agility, but even under a traditional work operating system, unions can offer advantages. UPS delivers its packages globally with more than 250,000 unionized drivers in the Teamsters Package Division. The UPS-Teamsters relationship is not without contention, but they have worked together for over eighty years, and many top UPS executives began as unionized drivers. This long-running UPS-Teamsters relationship offers advantages when the union can explain the rationale for difficult decisions such as workforce reductions or work location changes. The union can lobby policy makers to consider UPS for favorable trade, tax, or other advantages, based on its support of worker collectivity.

The future of unions and worker collectives may well include a vital role in platform-based work.[33] Just as UPS reveals the benefit of union collaboration, the "Hollywood model" offers important insights from an industry that has thrived for almost one hundred years with unionized contractors as their pivotal talent. For entertainment companies, their pivotal talent—like actors, directors, and production crews—are contractors who are also union members of the Screen Actors Guild (SAG) or American Federation of Television and Radio Artists (AFTRA). So, they are not managed by HR but instead by the general counsel or procurement. How can HR delegate the management of such pivotal talent? It can do so because in Hollywood, rules that would typically be set individually by the HR function in each company are instead formalized and standardized in the union contracts that span workers and organizations.

For example, when must a production use a qualified stunt driver? It's in the SAG/AFTRA "Stunt & Safety Digest":[34]

1. When any or all wheels will leave the driving surface
2. When tire traction will be broken, i.e., skids, slides, etc.
3. Impaired driver vision

It makes no sense for individual employers to codify Hollywood production requirements. Production crews don't have the time to learn new rules whenever they change employers. Adam Davidson describes the movie set of *The Big Short*: "The team had never worked together before. . . . And yet there was no transition time; everybody worked together seamlessly, instantly. They just got to work, and somehow it all fit together."[35] All of this occurs without an HR business partner in sight. For consistency across projects and employers, the rules must reflect the work, not employment. In Hollywood, unions keep the common rules.

For example, CAPS Payroll provides payroll services to movie and entertainment projects, with real-time web-based applications that directors and producers use during actual shooting.[36] Hollywood union contracts are a source of the rules underpinning these apps. As work evolves, HR leaders may find unions to be an unexpected source and common repository of the new work rules.

Traditional unions have seen their influence and membership decline for decades. More recently, there are signs that workers' desire for collective voice may be manifesting in renewed organizing of traditional unions in technology companies such as Google and among warehouse and other workers at Amazon. Even more interesting are new forms of collective voice that harness emerging social media to bring attention to grievances. Even with no union, social media and press coverage of workers' stories about working conditions, health and safety, or sexual harassment can go viral, amplifying the voice of one or a few into a broad collective movement. As the new work operating system deconstructs traditional ideas such as jobs, jobholders, and qualifications, both organizations and traditional unions may need to rethink the fundamental idea of employee voice.

The New Work Operating System and Education: Stackable Credentials

We have shown how powerfully the new work operating system can redefine and support workers by allowing the focus to shift from the worker as a jobholder to the worker as a whole person with a wide array of current and potential capabilities. Chapter 4 noted that the new work operating system offers opportunities to better capture the "whole person" and their full array of capabilities, not only those related to one job or a job progression.

This opportunity also calls for a similar shift in the way organizations and learning providers consider pathways from education to work. It means shifting from a focus on worker education as degrees to a focus on deconstructed learning and capabilities.

This obviously portends fundamental shifts in how education is conceived and delivered and in the relationship between education providers and organizations that engage and hire their students. For decades, education providers such as universities and community colleges have recognized the limits of the traditional system of a stable array of course offerings bundled into stable degrees. Such a system is often slow to respond to changes in what organizations need. Education institutions are structured with revenue based on the number of students taking courses in a virtual or physical certificate program, frequently offered on a physical campus until the students fulfill their degree. Professors and other staff are organized and provided incentives to deliver a stable set of classes that meet a stable set of degree requirements.

The mismatch between the traditional educational approach and the fast-changing requirements of agile organizations has motivated some organizations to offer their own training programs or "academies," where they deconstruct learning into modules that focus specifically on the skills they need and can be modified as needs change. Innovative approaches to "pathways" from education to work include platforms that use AI to translate the language of educational classes and degrees into the language of the work qualifications listed by employers. They also include partnerships, often at the local level, between community education providers and community companies in which the partners collaborate to redefine the education programs so that they better fit the company needs.

It is beyond this book to offer a full treatment on how education and lifelong learning must evolve to meet the challenges and opportunities of the new work operating system. However, the power and challenges of deconstruction for education is nicely illustrated by one innovative idea: stackable credentials.

During the COVID-19 pandemic, a *Wired* magazine article highlighted an increasingly popular approach to education, driven in part by the accelerated increase in virtual learning and online class offerings at universities, community colleges, and other institutions.[37] The article noted that the economic toll of the pandemic gave "microcredentials" a burst of momentum because "a lot of people will need more education to get back into the workforce, and they'll need to get it quickly, at the lowest possible cost, and in subjects directly relevant to available jobs."

In practice, the idea of stackable credentials is to deconstruct a traditional college degree into the component capabilities embedded within that degree. Students can then present their degree in terms of the deconstructed capabilities they have achieved, making it easier for employers and others to match their progress in the degree program to the deconstructed tasks/projects for which organizations need workers. Liberating the deconstructed capabilities from the bundle called a degree not only allows more precise matching of candidates to work, but it also opens up the possibility that educational attainment can be perpetually deconstructed and reinvented to meet changing needs.

Eventually, students can choose to "stack" sufficient credentials to actually earn the college degree. However, earning the degree does not require a continuous educational experience in which a fixed set of classes are taken in sequence. With the deconstructed credentials, students may move in and out of a degree program, perhaps using some of the credentials to take on a job or project, and then return to stack up more credentials and so on.

As one student featured in the *Wired* magazine article put it, "Even if I chose not to finish, I would still have these pieces and I'd say, 'Look what I've done,' as opposed to, 'I have two years of college' but nothing to show for it." This student stacked up high-demand industry certifications in subjects such as technical support, cloud technology, and data analysis while on her way to a bachelor's degree in data management.

The *Wired* article pointed out that according to the National Student Clearinghouse Research Center, more than a quarter of students in conventional college programs quit after their first year,[38] when a degree still seems intimidatingly far off. Many quit because more than 40 percent of bachelor's degree candidates don't finish in six years.[39] Students may run out of money or experience personal problems that sidetrack or slow them down. The longer they spend in school, the more likely they are to quit with no credentials at all despite their investment of time and money. Earning credentials on the way to earning a degree provides a series of rewards that may encourage students to persist. Even if they don't finish the degree, they have something to fall back on that can help them get a job (or an alternative work arrangement). Some evidence also suggests that students pursuing degrees that are deconstructed into microcredentials are more likely to finish the degree and are less likely to drop out after the first year.

Just as the new work operating system requires rethinking work and workers within organizations, it also requires rethinking learning and learners outside of organizations, in the context of the education ecosystem. The educational ecosystem faces similarly significant challenges to those we have described as organizations rethink their work operating system. However, the promise of integrating deconstructed work and workers within organizations with deconstructed degrees and learners in the education system holds immense opportunities to solve perennially thorny challenges for both.

Solving both challenges will also require attention to significant policy issues that can encourage and support innovations such as stackable credentials. Evelyn Ganzglass of the Center for Postsecondary and Economic Success noted these requirements:[40]

Create a common language for workplace and educational credentials. Industry and professional certifications describe mastery of competencies in the language of the workplace, but credit-bearing educational credentials describe course completion using college credits. If the languages of the workplace and educational institutions were more common, the deconstructed elements could be better matched and compared. Some have called these translations "crosswalks," which helps students, educators, job seekers, and the government understand what these credentials actually represent and promotes portability across boundaries.

Integrate education institutional governance. Governance arrangements affect how credentials are awarded and transferred between educational institutions and degrees. Such credential transference can be impeded by systems with disconnected authority over different educational entities such as community and technical colleges, four-year institutions, elementary and secondary education, adult education, and career and technical education. Similar disconnects can exist with state governance bodies, regional accreditors, colleges, and faculty curriculum committees within colleges. For example, technical diplomas and applied associate's degrees are often not transferrable to bachelor's degrees unless they are part of an applied baccalaureate degree.

Bridge silos between and inside educational institutions. Institutional silos include divisions between and within academic and occupational programs and the disciplines within them. Elective credits may not be fully transferrable and may not replace required courses from one program to another because the receiving institution determines whether and how many credits will transfer. If institutions could bridge and integrate disparate discipline-based course numbering conventions and jurisdiction, they could more easily create interdisciplinary programs that are key to lattice credentials that allow people to advance along multiple pathways.

Overcome the disconnect between credit and noncredit offerings. Many occupational training programs, even those provided by accredited educational institutions, are offered on a noncredit basis. This is often done to bypass the traditional academic approval process, which can be cumbersome and lengthy. Because noncredit courses don't count toward a degree, they can become dead-ends for student progress. One option is to get "credit for prior learning," but that is also a complicated and frequently costly process. Bridging this divide might mean negotiating credit arrangements for programs that combine occupational training with noncredit courses, including adult education and developmental education.

Provide financial aid for deconstructed credentials, not only degrees. Financial aid is frequently tied to traditional units such as semesters, courses, hours, or degrees. In the United States, federal financial aid requires a minimum number of weeks and clock or credit hours. Pell Grants are based on the number of completed semesters. Students without a high school diploma or equivalency or who were homeschooled are less eligible for federal financial aid. Educational institutions offering nondegree credentials are often required to prepare students for gainful employment in a recognized occupation, which reinforces a focus on jobs and traditional careers. Rules limit financial aid eligibility to 150 percent of the credits needed to complete a degree, diploma, or certificate program, which is a barrier to pathways that include courses that are required for a specific job but are not a part of the degree program.

Balance local flexibility with greater consistency and portability of credentials. Local flexibility to create short-term credentials has allowed colleges to respond quickly to specific employer needs and get students into the labor market, but it also creates discrepancies in the content and credits for these courses. Aligning these local programs with national certification standards would offer greater consistency, more portability, and a better connection to subsequent credentials along a career pathway.

Optimize and integrate the mix of learning in traditional classrooms, online, and experience. Certification standards usually focus on acquiring knowledge, performing relevant technical skills, and applying it to specific circumstances. Knowledge application is often best accomplished through practice in real working situations, so optimally combining these different elements of certification means incorporating internships and short-term work assignments (perhaps called "learning gigs") into the pedagogy models and course sequences in education institutions. Again, deconstruction, translation, and reinvention are key and must occur at the more granular level of capabilities and tasks, not degrees and jobs.

Virtually every organization recognizes that its agility is enhanced with a robust approach to things like reskilling and upskilling. Virtually all employers and education providers recognize the need for a stronger and more transparent connection between education and work, yet both organizations and education providers often try to accomplish these goals within the legacy framework of degrees, certificates, jobs, and jobholders. The new work operating system, based on deconstruction and reinvention, illuminates new options and opportunities to address these challenges more effectively.

New Work Operating System for the "100-Year Life"

In their book *The 100-Year Life*, Lynda Gratton and Andrew Scott propose that the traditional three-phase life (education, employment, retirement) will be replaced by a series of shorter stages, a mix of traditional working patterns, entrepreneurship, further education, concurrent part-time roles, and so on.[41] They suggest that work may need to continue into a person's eighties to accumulate the financial resources necessary for a comfortable lifestyle. While this might seem disappointing to those who favor the traditional prospect of fully retiring from the workforce at age sixty-five, Gratton and Scott propose that it can actually be seen as a source of greater fulfillment as workers age if it is paired with continuing reinvention through what the authors call "a repeating cycle of education, employment and retirement."

Such reinvention requires the new work operating system we have described here, but it also requires substituting our idea of "work" for the notion of "employment," our idea of deconstructed capabilities/skills for education and our idea of "work reinvention" for retirement. It requires a system where workers are not bound by their roles as jobholder and are free to grow and employ their deconstructed skills and capabilities, and where work is not bound up in finding a traditional job with a single employer but its deconstructed tasks can be pursued independently and offers far more options to step into and out of these three phases, perhaps even pursuing two of them at the same time.

Deloitte offers this scenario that illustrates the positive potential of the new work operating system, in this case through freelancing:

Tom spent nearly 40 years as a corporate executive in the financial services industry. His career was marked by much success, as he advised clients on the numbers behind potential mergers and acquisitions. But after the financial crisis, at age 62, he was forced into early retirement. Being financially savvy, Tom was well ahead of his peers when it came to his retirement fund, so he decided to take a year off and move closer to his grandchildren. He spent a lot of time on the road during his career and didn't want to miss out on his grandchildren growing up. But after a year, Tom found himself with too much time on his hands and not enough connection with the outside world. His adult children talked him into joining a freelancing platform as a gig worker. Tom could work only when he wanted to, have a chance to connect with others, and share the skills he built over his career, not to mention making some extra spending money for that family cruise he was planning. This gig work would allow him the flexibility and connection he was looking for post-career. It's not the money, he explains, but the flexibility and opportunity to connect with others that keeps him going.[42]

Of course, this scenario presumes that Tom was "ahead of the game" in funding his "retirement," and that allowed him the flexibility that comes with financial security, to focus on making new connections and learning new skills. Statistics show that most workers are hardly so fortunate and have not amassed such financial resources. Making such a future available widely and equitably will require enhancing social safety nets for workers and designing those safety nets so that they are portable and independent of the traditional regular full-time job. As Gratton and Scott warned, it is quite difficult to "try to get a mortgage without a steady income. Or to save for your retirement with an irregular salary and no employer's contributions."[43]

While social challenges exist in both the old and the new work operating system, it seems unlikely that the old work operating system of work as a job with an employment contract, and work-related protections only for "employees," can support longer lifespans that require repeated cycles of education-employment-retirement for seventy or more years. The difference between longer lives spent in exploitive work relationships versus spent in a flourishing and rewarding work ecosystem may well be whether societies embrace the new work operating system and redefine their definition of "employment security" and "employment protections" to encompass deconstruction.

Conclusions and Next Steps

You can see why many of the significant global and social and policy challenges both require and can support the new work operating system that frees the work from the confines of jobs and frees the worker from the confines of "jobholder." An increasing array of work either has already shifted (such as the tasks now posted to your internal talent marketplace or tasks you obtain through freelance platforms), will soon shift (such as work that is being combined with automation, work that has become remote, or where your traditional job descriptions have a short half-life), or *should* shift to the new work operating system, even if not all workers and leaders see it yet (such as work where it is difficult to find qualified workers, where development and career paths seem stuck, or where there is pressure to offshore or outsource).

The earlier chapters of this book have shown you how to identify what work offers the greatest return from shifting to the new work operating system as well as the steps to implementing it. Let's review the main frameworks and how they fit together.

1. Adopt the work design principles as a touchstone for all your efforts:
   * Start with the work (current and future tasks) and not the existing jobs.
   * Combine humans and automation and do not replace humans with automation.
   * Consider the full array of work engagements (e.g., employment, gig, freelance, alliances, projects, other alternative work arrangements), not just regular full-time employment.
   * Allow talent flow to work not be limited to fixed, traditional jobs.

2. Follow the new work operating system change process:
   - Start by identifying a high-value trigger for creating a prototype that will illustrate the power and value of the new work operating system. Typical triggers include operating challenges, constraints (like bottlenecks in processes or talent pipelines), new technology, and shifts in organizational priorities.
   - Ensure you have the right metrics in place to measure success.
3. Deploy the new work operating system:
   a. Deconstruct job elements (tasks):
      i. Answer the key guiding questions to begin the deconstruction process.
      ii. Deconstruct jobs and workflows.
   b. Automate work to optimize task-level combinations of human and automated work:
      i. Based on the deconstruction, determine the relevant role of automation.
      ii. Determine the relevant type of automation.
   c. Work arrangements include a boundaryless and democratized work ecosystem:
      i. Using the output from the deconstruction step, determine how widely the work can be dispersed and how far from employment it can be detached.
      ii. Determine the best way to connect talent to work (fixed roles, flow to work, or hybrid roles).
   d. Workers as a whole person with deconstructed capabilities versus as jobholders:
      i. Analyze the unique bundle of skills that comprise the "whole" person.
      ii. Map skills to tasks and construct logical skill progressions to enable talent development.
   e. Perpetually reinvented task combinations and diverse work arrangements define work:
      i. Sustain the new work operating system through the five core elements of process, culture, structure, people, and technology.

    ii. Leverage the principles of Agile to perpetually reinvent the new work operating system.

  f. Coordinate management and work as collaborative hubs of teams and projects, aligned goals/purpose and integrated through human/AI platforms and HR systems:

    i. Leverage AI to transform work coordination.

    ii. Approach work design as collaborative agile innovation.

    iii. Encourage perpetual work crafting and value negotiation.

    iv. Equip leaders/managers to shift from hierarchy to influence.

    v. Reinvent HR as a hub for agile work design innovation.

  g. Support and embody values and social policies that enable and rely on fluid work arrangements and holistic worker capability to achieve worker sustainability, voice, equity, and inclusion:

    i. Encourage social safety nets that make worker benefits more portable.

    ii. Use your market power to encourage work platforms to adhere to sustainable labor practices.

    iii. Collaborate with educational institutions to improve learning deconstruction and clearer common translations across learning credentials.

The New Work Operating System in Action at Providence Health and Services

Providence Health & Services is a nonprofit, Catholic health system operating multiple hospitals across eight states, with headquarters in Renton, Washington. The health system includes fifty-one hospitals, more than eight hundred nonacute facilities, and numerous other health, supportive housing, and educational services in the West Coast (Alaska, Washington, Oregon, and California) and Idaho, Montana, New Mexico, and Texas. Providence Health & Services was founded by the Sisters of Providence in 1859. Both before and during the COVID-19 crisis of 2020–2021, Providence Health was dedicated to solving thorny strategic and workforce issues creatively. Many of their innovations are good illustrations of the new work system in action.

Earlier chapters have alluded to some of the Providence work innovations. Here, we describe the Providence experience more fully to comprehensively show how its work innovations reflect each of the elements of the new work operating system.

Focus on Pivotal Strategic Goals, Processes, or External Challenges that Make Traditional Work Nonoptimal

There are several seismic shifts happening in healthcare that are dramatically shaping how the work is performed and, in turn, how the workforce itself needs to be organized and equipped to do the work. A few of these shifts include the advancement of technology, changing consumer expectations, and evolving governmental regulations and priorities. Another significant driver is the global gap in the supply and demand of healthcare talent, exacerbated by the aging population. Simply put, the demand for healthcare is skyrocketing at the same time a huge percentage of the healthcare workforce is retiring. As Greg Till, Providence's chief people officer, explains, "It's challenging enough to find the talent needed to fill roles today. It is going to be impossible in a few years. There's no way to hire, develop, and retain our way into the future. Continuing to practice the way we always have isn't only nonoptimal, it's not plausible. We need to innovate how the work is performed, for the benefit of the caregivers themselves and our communities."

With this premise, Till and Mark Smith, Providence's head of workforce strategy and analytics, partnered with clinical, operations, human resources, and finance leaders to imagine what the future of work at Providence might look like. While this work started several years ago, the COVID-19 pandemic dramatically accelerated progress, and the work started prior to COVID-19 enabled Providence to lead the way.

Work as Deconstructed Job Elements (Tasks, Activities, Projects)

When beginning their exploration into the future of work, Providence started with the premise that any changes wouldn't just have to benefit patients and their communities; they should also make a meaningful impact on their employees, who Providence calls "caregivers," whether they are in clinical or administrative roles. Providences culture promotes finding "meaning in work," where their caregivers feel "called" to their vocations and can bring their "whole selves" to work.

As Providence began to deconstruct the job of a nurse, they observed that the nursing job contained some tasks that were "top of license," meaning they required and drew upon the unique high-level capabilities that characterized nursing training and tasks. However, the job had evolved to also contain a significant amount of time and many tasks that did not draw upon nor require the unique capabilities of a fully trained nurse. In addition to contributing to excess costs, "below license" work also results in lower engagement and less job satisfaction. The following table depicts the tasks that typically fall into each classification:

Top of license	Below license
• As part of a multidisciplinary care team, creating coordinated treatment plans for patients	• Less complex diagnostic assessment (blood pressure, temperature checking, injections, etc.)
• Conducting or assisting with complex clinical procedures (e.g., intubation)	• Documentation (patient charting, manual or in an electronic medical record)
• Compassionately providing emotional support for patients and families	• "Sitting"—providing patients in need of supervision with companionship and care
• Simplifying complex issues so patients can make the best decisions	• Nonclinical training
• Training patients to care for themselves after discharge	• Attending meetings

Nurses were spending over 35 percent of their time on below license asks. While this situation might have been acceptable at a time when healthcare was stable and there was an adequate supply of nurses, it had become evident that in a changing health care environment and massive nurse shortages, the organization could ill-afford to have its nurses spending time on tasks that did not require their unique capabilities. It also wasn't consistent with Providence's effort to create a "best place to work and practice." The COVID-19 crisis accelerated this imperative, as hospitals were increasingly operating at full capacity or beyond and where the difference between life and death could rest upon innovations to deploy key talent precisely where it was needed.

In addition to nurses, Providence has used the idea of deconstructing jobs in several other areas. Over the past several years, for instance, the team has dramatically lowered administrative costs and transformed work in an effort, called "Accelerating to Health 2.0." This project focused on modernizing work and reducing variation, like a lot of other transformation efforts. However, it also encouraged shared services leaders to review every job and ask which tasks could be automated, eliminated, simplified, or done with better value using a different approach (done as part of a different role, using an external partner, performed in a different location, etc.).

Many of these efforts were accelerated further when Providence's administrative team, and many of its clinicians, moved to working remotely. As with most organizations, Providence discovered new insights about what tasks might be done remotely and how to keep caregivers fully engaged, connected, and productive while working from home. It found many more work elements that could be done offsite than they had previously imagined, and their surveys showed that newly remote workers' engagement had actually increased by nine points (an unheard-of increase in one year). As a result, Providence leaders and caregivers were already rethinking work and organization design and were carefully analyzing the division of time between working on site versus remotely. This analysis required deconstructing jobs into components and then reinventing the work to reflect new lessons in on-site versus remote work. For example, employees became comfortable interacting remotely with HR advisors who were previously always available in person, and this accelerated using chatbots to answer simple employee questions and shifting such questions to a centralized call center in the Philippines. Certain tasks in the hiring process that were previously done in person (benefits enrollment, I-9s, and other necessary legal and tax forms) were now shifted to a virtual approach.

Work deconstruction and reinvention extended to a key job within the HR function itself. The work of employee relations—helping resolve workplace issues with employees—had always been seen as "high touch." So it was historically presumed that it must be done "locally" as a vital component of the job of every local HR business partner (HRBP).

During the pandemic, as everything from general health visits to new hire orientation went virtual, Providence deconstructed and reinvented the HRBP role. Many HRBP tasks had already been automated, out-sourced, or centralized but not employee relations. Deconstructing the HRBP job revealed that the tasks of employee relations were now taking time away from other "higher license" HRBP work, such as connecting talent strategies with growth plans, leading change, or cultivating highly engaged, high-performing leadership teams. Moreover, employee relations work had become more legally and technically demanding. Thus distributing employee relations work to every HRBP created high variability, increased organizational risk, dissatisfaction among managers and employees, and other concerns.

The "change ready" environment COVID-19 created inspired Providence HR to deconstruct and reinvent employee relations. Taking a page from Providence's telehealth services, HR deconstructed and removed employee relations from the HRBP job. It created new jobs within a centralized team that now handles tiered employee relations issues virtually. This team can perform their work from any location and now follows a standard intake process, receives formal training, and is supported by a CRM tool.

This change shifted 25–35 percent of low-level tasks from the HRBP job, allowing them to spend more time on strategic efforts. In addition, isolating and centralizing the employee relations tasks led to quicker and more consistent issue resolution, higher levels of satisfaction, and reduced mistakes and risk. As Till put it, "By deconstructing the HRBP role and reconstructing the employee relations component differently, the HR team and the employees they support can now have it fast, cheap, and good!"

Work Automation as Optimizing Task-Level Combinations of Human and Automated Work

A significant amount of below license work benefited from Providence's investments in technology and automation over the last several years. Led by a digital innovations group, Providence presents several examples of the human-automation connection that Providence leaders described as "the intersection between compassion and innovation":

- *Patient engagement* is aided by technology that uses automation to enhance the direct communication between providers and patients, when they're at home.
- *Diagnostics* have been dramatically enabled by technology, like IRIS (interferometric reflectance imaging sensor), which can detect diabetes early using a retinal scan.
- *Pharmaceutical delivery* is now enhanced with automation that provides efficient management of inventory and easier drug delivery.
- *Administrative tasks*, like scheduling, referrals, scribing, and payment processing, have been dramatically simplified with automation.
- Smith's team at Providence is currently piloting the automation of nursing schedules, posting of roles ahead of demand, and even offering optimal unit designs to optimize outcomes for caregivers, patients, and communities. Providence is implementing a system of *predictive scheduling*. Using technology that retrieves data from multiple platforms (timekeeping systems, electronic medical record systems), the workforce optimization team will be able to forecast hourly staffing demand in every department across Providence's family of organizations and run this information through decision optimization software that delivers rapid, dynamic schedules to leaders. The software completes optimization in about three minutes, replacing a manual process used by the workforce optimization team that previously took about twelve hours to complete.
- *Virtual visits*, which have skyrocketed through COVID-19, have benefited from automated patient navigation.

Work Arrangements Include a Boundaryless and Democratized Work Ecosystem

As is typical in healthcare, Providence has a long history of using workers engaged in ways other than regular full-time employment. Before COVID-19, these included agency nurses, contractors, volunteers, and part-time workers. Some of these relationships are in place based on legal governance (e.g., hospital systems can't employ physicians in California). Others are used to provide temporary capacity to support demand fluctuations or fill short-term capability gaps, and others are contracted to perform certain below license tasks. While many components of the nursing role could be optimized through deconstruction and reconstruction, several factors had prevented full realization of this vision, including talent availability (certified nursing assistants (CNAs) and medical assistants were almost as scarce as nurses), legal constraints (e.g., licensure laws), contractual constraints, technology gaps, or change readiness.

With the onset of the COVID-19 crisis, the organization expanded its aperture to include retirees, nursing students still in college, and those who had previously left a full-time job at Providence but were willing to return as gig workers. It also initiated short-term rotations in apprenticeship roles to prepare people for future high-demand opportunities such as being a medical assistant, CNA, registered nurse, or pharmacy technician. Providence employed a variety of tactics during COVID-19 to engage talent, and the table below describes those tactics within the framework of this book.

In addition to the recent innovation, and throughout the COVID-19 pandemic, Providence has been working for several years to create a talent system that constantly looks at job tasks to assess what work can be performed more effectively through automation, partnerships (on shore and off), gig workers, or other, more appropriately positioned caregivers.

A good example of this evolution is the changing role of CNAs. A significant portion of what CNAs do today, for instance, used to be performed by nurses. Hospital CNAs provide direct patient care in

New work operating system elements	Providence examples
Deconstructing the internal talent marketplace (chapter 1)	• Developed labor pool to identify staffing needs during COVID-19 surges and matched caregiver skills to immediate staffing needs • Used "redeployment teams" to effectively move caregivers from lower-demand units to higher-demand units • Allowed exempt caregivers to flow to where they were needed most, even across state lines, to address COVID-19 spikes and vaccination efforts
Automating (robots/AI) (chapter 2)	• Partnered with a vendor to pilot autoscribe so providers had access to voice-captured notetaking • Massively expanded use of virtual visits (telehealth) to engage with patients via the internet from the comfort and safety of their homes; virtual visits increased from 67,000 in 2019 to more than 1.6 million visits in 2020. • Infused AI and RPA in hiring, compensation, payroll, accounts payable, supply chain, and other administrative processes. Launched chatbots in service centers.
Tapping nonemployee talent sources (chapter 3)	• Developed service-level agreements with unaffiliated medical practices to employ their staff in hospitals requiring additional staffing • Enlisted services from retired nurses to staff vaccination clinics • Used temporary staff to greet patients, take temperatures, and do other work typically performed by nurses or other clinicians • Employed contract nurses to deal with demand surges, strikes, and talent shortages • Developed creative staffing agency agreements to provide services for traditional and nontraditional rotations • Enlisted qualified interns at vaccination clinics • Patient attendant apprentices served as patient sitters to allow nurses to focus efforts on critical patients
Uncovering hidden nursing capabilities in nonnursing roles (chapter 4)	• Implemented caregiver skills identification inventory on the performance management platform • Mapped caregivers' capabilities beyond their job descriptions • Recertified nursing task capabilities among senior hospital administrators

New work operating system elements	Providence examples
Perpetually reinventing work to meet surges and changing needs (chapter 5)	• Implemented predictive hiring using AI to predict work demand months in advance • Flowed newly recertified administrators to the nursing floor to meet unexpected surges in care demand • Created a new role, "support service tech," adding point-of-entry monitoring tasks to jobs in delivery, transport, stocking, and cleaning
Building collaborative cross-functional leadership (chapter 6)	• Solutions Center identified emerging needs and brought together HR, clinical, nursing, and operations leaders to develop new ways to effectively meet challenges • Automated schedule creation, staffing and demand management, preposting for predicted vacancies, integrated resource management, and so on, all aimed at helping nurse supervisors shift nurses to work at the top of their license • Eliminated or redistributed nonessential management and supervisory tasks, allowing more time to support caregivers
Seeding innovations outside the organization (chapter 7)	• Established a venture fund that invests in companies to help innovate and accelerate new combinations of human and automated work

coordination with nurses. They respond to patient call lights; help move, clean, and feed bedridden patients; monitor blood pressure and vital signs; ensure their patients take in enough nourishment at mealtime; and often serve as sitters, staying with patients who require a higher level of observation. One hospital saw a dramatic increase in sitter use, requiring nurses and CNAs to perform those duties. As the demand for CNAs rose sharply to address the nursing supply shortage, CNAs also became difficult to staff. Providence responded by deconstructing the CNA's role, asking what specific tasks and activities could be performed by student nurse assistants. This led to the creation of a "patient attendant" role, which was able to meet a good portion of the sitter needs and provide a pipeline of CNAs for the future. Becoming a patient attendant involves a sixteen-week rotation of training, test preparation, and CNA-related work in preparation to convert to a full-time CNA role. One key task is serving as a sitter. The task is within the scope of patient attendant work and allows CNAs (and nurses) to perform more complex tasks. This new role provides meaningful career opportunities for current caregivers and individuals who previously had limited access to healthcare careers. Externally, the patient attendant role offers the vulnerable, underemployed population an opportunity for sustainable employment.

Workers as a "Whole Person," with an Array of Deconstructed Capabilities (e.g., Skills, Competencies, Abilities)

Perhaps the most vivid example of the new work operating system came as Providence mapped caregivers' capabilities beyond their job descriptions. As Smith said, "Our focus on jobs meant that we didn't understand skills."

Because nursing tasks were identified as the most pivotal bottleneck, Providence first set out to find untapped sources of talent for these tasks, regardless of the job description. A survey was created listing the skills, capabilities, and certifications for tasks customarily done by nurses. Each caregiver, both clinical and nonclinical, was asked to complete the survey, noting which of the skills, capabilities, or certifications they held.

A case study by i4cp in 2021 noted that Providence's internal marketplace was supported with both human and automated work.[1] Providence assembled an internal talent marketplace committee comprised of seventy-five people representing every healthcare facility. This committee assessed needs across the system and ensured each facility had caregivers with skills needed to meet dynamic demand. The committee initially met several times per week to review the status of each site. A smaller team then took this input and developed a "red/yellow/green" assessment. Workers with needed skills were deployed to sites forecasted to be red or yellow (immediate or near immediate need).

The result was the first comprehensive "library" of capabilities for the tasks typically performed in the nursing job. This library supported three key tasks:

1. Identify caregivers in any role that were able to perform top of license nursing tasks. Initially, you might think that these tasks would be exclusively assigned to nurses. However, the process of searching for deconstructed capabilities revealed that hospital administrators and managers had often risen through the ranks of nursing or were doctors. For these individuals, their jobs of administrator or manager did not include nursing tasks, nor did they reflect nursing or physical capabilities. However, the individual holding the administrator or manager jobs still possessed those capabilities. Thus, these individuals were encouraged to renew their licenses and become eligible to do some amount of nursing and other tasks on the hospital floor in addition to their day job of administration or management. This revealed options that had previously been unknown or untapped by Providence leaders. As an example, the CEO of Providence's Southern California region realized that a significant number of his top hospital administrators could work eight hours per week on the hospital floor, providing a much-needed way to help alleviate the significant strains on hospitals during the COVID-19 crisis.

   This helped immensely through COVID-19 because typical staffing approaches were insufficient as demand dramatically spiked in some areas (e.g., respiratory therapy units) while plummeting in others (e.g., elective surgeries). It also helped when vaccines became available, as Providence has enlisted licensed executives, retired licensed nurses, and qualified interns to administer vaccinations in stand-up clinics across seven states. Even the CEO of Providence's Washington/ Montana region, a former nurse, took shifts administering vaccines. These efforts have led to some of the highest caregiver vaccination rates in the healthcare industry.[2]

2. Rapidly deploy entry-level or less skilled talent to "below license" tasks, like checking temperatures at hospital entries, expediting and

escorting patients and supplies to the point of care, and effectively managing, and in some cases building, personal protective equipment. In this regard, Providence considered what nonnursing caregivers might have capabilities to do those tasks, freeing up nurses for tasks where they were uniquely qualified.

For these tasks, it made sense to explore deploying them to nonnursing tasks, but the traditional work operating system had bundled work into jobs and workers into jobholders. So, it was difficult to unearth workers who might have the capability to take on some of the nonnursing tasks, let alone have the mechanisms to deploy those tasks into their existing jobs. Once the tasks and the necessary capabilities were deconstructed, it was more possible to envision moving some nonnursing tasks to others. For example, nurses spent a lot of time taking patient temperatures or stopping by to ask patients how they were doing. These tasks could be done by those in other jobs, such as receptionists and records administrators. A records administrator, for example, was already familiar with the chart entries needed when taking a patient's temperature or checking to see if they were responsive and feeling all right, so it was a small change for the same administrator to actually take the temperature or check in on the patient and fill in the chart entry. Hospital receptionists could also spend some time on the floor taking temperatures and recording the data. If the patient exhibited a high temperature or showed any signs of requiring attention, the administrator or receptionist could summon the nurse. This deconstruction revealed a surprising amount of nurse time that could be freed up by having others do such tasks.

Outside of nursing, another opportunity for deconstruction/reconstruction through COVID-19 occurred at hospital entry points. As hospitals limited visitors for safety reasons, there arose a need for entry-point monitoring. Rather than create a new role, several hospitals evaluated the expected skills for a door monitor and compared the skills to other positions in the facility. The hospital identified that at least six positions had similar skills requirements. This discovery led to the development of the support service tech, made up of skills identified in delivery, transport, stocking, and cleaning positions. Individuals in this role use their skills to perform a variety of related duties and provide the hospital greater flexibility in meeting patient care needs while addressing an emerging requirement to monitor entry points. Technology and easing of the pandemic may soon reduce the need for entry-point monitoring, but there remains a need to have the right people in the right place at the right time to meet patient needs. This role is seen by leadership, the labor union representing the roles, and caregivers as a gateway to other opportunities within the hospital.

3. Begin redesigning the nursing role, more strategically, for the future. In addition to finding other caregivers, who could take pieces of a nurse's role, a significant amount of effort was and is still being put in to finding ways to eliminate nonvalue-added tasks from the nurse's role or to innovate new ways of performing tasks that can't be completely removed. One example of this includes compliance training. Compliance training is below license but is necessary for obvious reasons. In 2019, Providence implemented a technology, called Qstream, taking an average annual load of four hours' worth of compliance training and condensing it into a series of knowledge-based questions caregivers get pushed to their mobile phones (or work computers). This simple innovation has not only reduced the amount of time annual compliance activities take by over 90 percent, but it has also increased the training's effectiveness. At Providence's scale, this represents over 150,000 hours of time a nurse can now spend time doing more meaningful, satisfying top of license tasks.

Perpetually Reinvented Task/Project Combinations, Work Arrangements, and "Flow to the Work"

Once jobs are deconstructed, it is much easier to imagine solutions that involve reinventing work so that it spans individuals from different jobs or others where workers can flow to a work priority that might not have been part of their job in the traditional system.

The exemplars above involving clinical and nonclinical caregivers flowing to areas experiencing COVID-19 spikes or engaging in the single task of administering vaccines to accelerate distribution provide good examples of flowing to the work. Once the capability set of these administrators and managers was identified and their licenses were renewed, an additional ongoing solution was to have them work eight hours per week on the floor or more where necessary. Knowing they were qualified should an unexpected surge in demand occur provides one more avenue to ensure full support for patients, communities, and overworked caregivers. In that case, a task was added to their existing role to attend to the surge in demand.

While this was immensely helpful during COVID-19 and provides an additional option for unexpected demand spikes in the future, it might not be practical or affordable as a long-term solution. The solution that will be sustainable long term is the idea and practice of perpetually reinventing work in a way that both continues to create more meaning and connection for employees and creates more value for organizations and consumers. While this concept has been around for over one hundred years (CNAs have been supporting nurses since World War 1, though less than fifty years ago, only certified nurses were qualified to measure blood pressure), Providence started accelerating efforts to reinvent jobs two-and-a-half years ago as it became clear it was the best path meet current and future challenges. Till and Smith call this "bringing our future to the present."

Leadership, Management, and Coordination through Collaborative Hubs of Teams and Projects

The new work operating system at Providence required individual leaders and managers to rethink their own work, reinventing it to include such things as spending eight hours per week on the hospital floor doing tasks formerly bundled into the nurse job. However, the new work operating system also requires deeper changes in the fundamental role of leaders and managers. Once jobs and jobholders are deconstructed, and workers may flow to the work beyond their formal job assignment, subordinates are no longer restricted to their former jobs, in which they reported exclusively to only one manager or leader.

For example, imagine that you are the manager who supervises receptionists who now leave their reception desk to check on patients or take temperatures. How much precedence should you give to the two different tasks? How flexible should you be about allowing the receptionist to take time away when the nurse on the hospital floor makes an urgent request?

As another example, imagine that you are the CEO of the Southern California region, and you have now announced your support for having your high-level administrators renew their medical practice licenses so that they can spend eight hours per week on the hospital floor, assisting in things like giving injections? How will you decide what are the eight hours per week? How will you coordinate the needs and wishes of your executives as they work to meet your laudable goal? Will you establish "core executive time" when everyone is to be available for collective meetings? Will you establish a shift scheduling arrangement that coordinates calendars to optimally combine the "executive" tasks with the "on the hospital floor" tasks?

It quickly became apparent to Providence executives that this management and coordination must be supported by innovation in arenas such as more automated and intelligent skills and capabilities assessments, organization and job design, workforce and task-related demand management, supervisor capability development, and a reimagining of traditional pay and performance management systems, all of which puts HR in a critical role to help drive value creation in the new operating system, both for employees and consumers.

The focus on reconstructing roles for individual contributors also has significant impact on supervisors. In addition to the complexities involved in a reimagined operating system noted above, supervisors too will need to have their roles deconstructed to ensure they can support the new ways of working in the best way possible. To prepare, Providence has also invested a significant amount of thought and resources to eliminating or redistributing the nonessential management tasks supervisors need to perform, allowing them more time to support their caregivers.

In the case of nurse managers, for instance, this means auto-opening requisitions before vacancies occur, using analytics to predict needs ahead of demand, and taking the manual effort out of scheduling. Recall that Providence automated "predictive scheduling." That system creates new opportunities for leaders and managers. Leaders will be able to use the software to make choices about how to build staffing schedules, reducing the time it takes to create a schedule from several hours to ten minutes. Where self-scheduling is available, caregivers will have the ability to select shifts that meet their needs. This system recommends skills needed throughout the day. In one sample build-up, an emergency department discovered that it needed to change its emergency department tech use to a one-to-four per-nurse ratio to optimize staff levels and ensure that nurses performed at top of license during daily peak patient influx.

The Providence HR Function Supports and Models the New Work Operating System

These leadership, management, and coordination changes are supported by the Providence HR team. The team has taken steps over the last several years to become an industry leader in innovative value creation. Some pioneering examples in healthcare include a creative partnership with IBM to enhance certain tasks in talent acquisition, payroll, and the HR Service Center, in some cases augmenting their US teams with talent overseas. It has also modeled a new centralized, virtual employee relations hub after the organization's telehealth model, helping resolve issues more quickly and effectively than ever before and moving more tasks from HR business partners to others. Providence HR is modeling the optimization of humans and automation, using AI and RPA in hiring, payroll, and service center activities (automating interview schedules, identifying better skills/task matches, making faster offers, streamlining payroll transactions, and using chatbots to answer simple caregiver questions during or after business hours).

One notable change for HR over the last several years, and exacerbated by COVID-19, was that to effectively deal with significant demand spikes and supply shortages, HR professionals needed to think about talent management more like manufacturing organizations think about their supply chains. In response, HR reimagined hiring as "demand management." For example, while it was well known for years that it could take six months to fill vacancies in high-demand areas, Providence leaders and their HR counterparts often waited until a vacancy arose to then attempt to fill a job description. HR implemented predictive hiring, where tools such as AI were used to predict work demand months in advance and to allow recruiters and others to start months early in order to create a pipeline to fill vacancies.

HR also was also quick to model efforts to flow to the work, designing a new Solutions Center concept based on deconstructed tasks rather than jobs. A small team of dedicated project managers helped manage immediate and urgent tasks by allowing those with the right skills to "bid" or volunteer to help on limited-time projects, effectively creating an internal talent market for gig workers with full-time jobs. This effort improved engagement while significantly improving capacity because caregivers got to choose how they wanted to use their "discretionary" time, based on their unique skills and what they felt "called" to do.

Final Words

The new work operating system may seem daunting at first. Once you realize that work can be usefully deconstructed into tasks and skills, there appear to be infinite combinations and massive issues to confront in your existing talent systems, process models, boundary relationships, and so on. That's why we recommend starting small, with one of the trigger points we described in the initial chapters. Start in places where the work evolution in your organization has already created recognition that the old operating system is insufficient and where there is energy to try something new. Then, create a prototype and use it to illustrate both the power of the new work operating system as well as how to foresee and overcome potential obstacles. It's helpful to focus first on the organization processes affected by the work, identify the process bottlenecks that could be overcome with a better approach to the work, and then derive the work implications.

Once the new work operating system takes hold, it will expand. Existing job descriptions and jobholder qualifications or competencies will soon seem ill-suited to the purpose of designing work of the future. There will be calls to expand the prototypes to more of the work and workforce as more stakeholders see the exponential gains possible with the new work operating system. Armed with your initial successes, you will be better prepared to guide this evolution strategically.

As we have shown in this book, there are tectonic shifts in the very definition of work and workers who go to the heart of the future work relationships. Technological and social disruptions have accelerated these shifts, and the pace will only increase. Even if today your traditional work operating system seems sufficient to the task, a careful look will reveal the "edges" where these work changes are already affecting your organization. Take the opportunity to understand and experiment with this new work operating system now, and you will be better prepared to face the vital challenges of the future. Moreover, you have the chance to create a more empowering, inclusive, agile, and proactive organization and to avoid the needless costs of reacting too late or opting for ill-suited traditional tactics. In the spirit of Agile, embrace and experiment with the new work operating system. The exponential gains and possibilities we have illustrated in this book are but the tip of the iceberg.

Acknowledgments

We are most grateful for the support of our many colleagues who inspired and challenged us in the writing of this book, including those at the Center for Effective Organizations, University of Southern California, i4cp, Mercer, and Willis Towers Watson.

We are particularly grateful to our colleagues at Mercer for their encouragement and support and greatly appreciate Ilya Bonic's thoughtful input. We also thank Willis Towers Watson and former colleagues Tracey Malcolm, Carole Hathaway, and Laurie Bienstock for their support and contributions.

We are most thankful for the generous counsel and insights of our manuscript reviewers and the great team at MIT Press, especially Kathleen Caruso and Paul Michelman. We are particularly grateful for the incredible patience and support from our editor Emily Taber whose coaching and insights made this book so much better.

Last, but by no means least, we are eternally grateful for the support and encouragement of our spouses, Maureen Jesuthasan and Megan Boudreau, without whom this book would never have been possible.

Notes

Introduction

1. Edie Goldberg and Kelley Steven-Waiss, *The Inside Gig: How Sharing Untapped Talent across Boundaries Unleashes Organizational Capacity* (Vancouver, BC, Canada: LifeTree Media, 2020).

2. John W. Boudreau, Ravin Jesuthasan, and David Creelman, *Lead the Work: Navigating a World beyond Employment* (Hoboken, NJ: John Wiley & Sons, 2015).

3. Boudreau, Jesuthasan, and Creelman, *Lead the Work*.

4. John W. Boudreau, "Why Work Platforms Are the Future for American Laborers," Resource Corner, February 27, 2017, https://www.cornerstoneondemand .com/rework/work-platform-new-%E2%80%9Cjob-displaced-workers.

5. "Politicians Cannot Bring Back Old-Fashioned Factory Jobs," *Economist*, January 14, 2017, http://www.economist.com/news/briefing/21714330-they-dont -make-em-any-more-politicians-cannot-bring-back-old-fashioned-factory-jobs.

6. Andrew Tangel, "Companies Plow Ahead with Moves to Mexico, despite Trump's Pressure," *Wall Street Journal*, February 8, 2017, https://www.wsj.com /articles/rexnord-plows-ahead-with-mexico-plans-despite-trumps-pressure -1486555201.

7. "Will the Pandemic Push Knowledge Work into the Gig Economy?," *Harvard Business Review*, June 1, 2020, https://hbr.org/2020/06/will-the-pandemic-push -knowledge-work-into-the-gig-economy.

8. "A Labor Market That Works: Connecting Talent with Opportunity in the Digital Age," McKinsey & Company, June 2015, https://www.mckinsey.com /~/media/McKinsey/Featured%20Insights/Employment%20and%20Growth /Connecting%20talent%20with%20opportunity%20in%20the%20digital%20

age/MGI%20Online%20talent_A_Labor_Market_That_Works_Executive_%20
summary_June%202015.ashx.

9. "COVID-19 Has Ushered in the 'Intangible Company': Here Are 4 Ways It Will Change Business," World Economic Forum, June 16, 2020, https://www.weforum .org/agenda/2020/06/covid-19-intangible-company-leadership-remote-working/.

10. Ravin Jesuthasan and John W. Boudreau, *Reinventing Jobs: A 4-Step Approach for Applying Automation to Work* (Boston, MA: Harvard Business Review Press, 2018); Boudreau, Jesuthasan, and Creelman, *Lead the Work*.

11. James Bessen, "Toil and Technology," Finance & Development, March 2015, International Monetary Fund, https://www.imf.org/external/pubs/ft/fandd/2015 /03/bessen.htm.

12. Thomas Heath, "Bank Tellers Are the Next Blacksmiths," *Washington Post*, February 8, 2017, https://www.washingtonpost.com/business/economy/bank-tellers-are-the -next-blacksmiths/2017/02/08/fdf78618-ee1c-11e6-9662-6eedf1627882_story.html.

13. Amber Murakami-Fester, "Why Bank Tellers Won't Become Extinct Any Time Soon," Daily Commercial, March 30, 2017, https://www.dailycommercial .com/business/20170330/why-bank-tellers-wont-become-extinct-any-time-soon.

14. Thomas Bailey and Clive R. Belfield, "Stackable Credentials: Awards for the Future?," Working paper no. 92, Columbia University Community College Research Center, 2017, 8, https://ccrc.tc.columbia.edu/publications/stackable -credentials-awards-for-future.html.

15. Boudreau, Jesuthasan, and Creelman, *Lead the Work*.

16. Richard Salame, "The New Taylorism," *Jacobin*, February 20, 2018, https:// www.jacobinmag.com/2018/02/amazon-wristband-surveillance-scientific-man agement.

17. Salame, "The New Taylorism."

18. William Bridges, "The End of the Job," *Fortune*, September 19, 1994.

19. Bridges, "The End of the Job."

20. Amy Wrzesniewski and Jane E. Dutton, "Crafting a Job: Revisioning Employees as Active Crafters of Their Work," *Academy of Management Review* 26, no. 2 (2001): 179–201.

21. Arnold B. Bakker and Evangelia Demerouti, "Job Demands-Resources Theory: Taking Stock and Looking Forward," *Journal of Occupational Health Psychology* 22, no. 3 (2017): 273–285.

22. Alessandra Lazazzara, Maria Tims, and Davide de Gennaro, "The Process of Reinventing a Job: A Meta–Synthesis of Qualitative Job Crafting Research," *Journal of Vocational Behavior* 116, no. 103267 (2020): 103267.

23. Richard Feloni, "Zappos' CEO Says This Is the Biggest Misconception People Have about His Company's Self-Management System," *Business Insider*, February 2, 2016, https://www.businessinsider.com/zappos-ceo-tony-hsieh-on-misconception-about-holacracy-2016-2.

24. Bourree Lam, "What Happened after Zappos Got Rid of Workplace Hierarchy," *Atlantic Monthly*, January 15, 2016, https://www.theatlantic.com/business/archive/2016/01/zappos-holacracy-hierarchy/424173/.

25. Christina DesMarais, "Your Employees Like Hierarchy (No, Really)," Inc., August 16, 2012, http://www.inc.com/christina-desmarais/your-employees-like-hierarchy-no-really.html.

26. "Jeffrey Pfeffer: Do Workplace Hierarchies Still Matter?," Stanford Graduate School of Business, March 24, 2014, https://www.gsb.stanford.edu/insights/jeffrey-pfeffer-do-workplace-hierarchies-still-matter; Jeffrey Pfeffer, "You're Still the Same: Why Theories of Power Hold over Time and across Contexts," *Academy of Management Perspectives* 27, no. 4 (2013): 269–280.

Chapter 1

1. Ravin Jesuthasan and John Boudreau, *Reinventing Jobs: A 4-Step Approach for Applying Automation to Work* (Boston, MA: Harvard Business Review Press, 2018).

2. John W. Boudreau, "Jobs Are Melting into Fluid Work," Center for Effective Organizations, September 29, 2020, https://ceo.usc.edu/2020/09/29/jobs-are-melting-jobs-into-fluid-work/.

3. John W. Boudreau, *Retooling HR: Using Proven Business Tools to Make Better Decisions about Talent* (Boston, MA: Harvard Business Review Press, 2014); John W. Boudreau and Ravin Jesuthasan, *Transformative HR: How Great Companies Use Evidence-Based Change for Sustainable Advantage* (Nashville, TN: John Wiley & Sons, 2011).

4. "The Future of Work after COVID-19," McKinsey Global Institute, February 18, 2021, https://www.mckinsey.com/featured-insights/future-of-work/the-future-of-work-after-covid-19#.

Chapter 2

1. "Luddite," Wikipedia, March 15, 2021, https://en.wikipedia.org/w/index.php?title=Luddite&oldid=1012207760.

2. "This Robot Scientist Conducted Experiments by Itself during COVID-19 Lockdown," World Economic Forum, August 4, 2020, https://www.weforum.org/agenda/2020/08/robot-scientist-experiments-covid-19-lockdown/.

3. "Tommy the Robot Nurse Helps Italian Doctors Care for COVID-19 Patients," TheWorld, April 8, 2020, https://www.pri.org/stories/2020-04-08/tommy-robot-nurse-helps-italian-doctors-care-covid-19-patients.

4. Evan Ackerman, "Autonomous Robots Are Helping Kill Coronavirus in Hospitals," IEEE Spectrum, March 11, 2021, https://spectrum.ieee.org/automaton/robotics/medical-robots/autonomous-robots-are-helping-kill-coronavirus-in-hospitals.

5. China Xinhua News (@XHNews), "Amid a Novel Coronavirus Outbreak, Robots Are Deployed to Deliver Meals to Travelers in Isolation at a Hotel in Hangzhou, China," Twitter, January 7, 2021, https://twitter.com/XHNews/status/1221782244525858819.

6. Pratik Jakhar, "Coronavirus: China's Tech Fights Back," BBC, March 3, 2020, https://www.bbc.com/news/technology-51717164.

7. Zak Doffman, "This New Coronavirus Spy Drone Will Make Sure You Stay Home," *Forbes Magazine*, March 5, 2020, https://www.forbes.com/sites/zakdoffman/2020/03/05/meet-the-coronavirus-spy-drones-that-make-sure-you-stay-home/.

8. "The Future Chief People Officer: Imagine. Invent. Ignite," Society for Human Resources Management, January 17, 2020, https://www.willistowerswatson.com/en-US/Insights/2020/01/the-future-chief-people-officer-imagine-invent-ignite.

9. Ravin Jesuthasan and John W. Boudreau, *Reinventing Jobs: A 4-Step Approach for Applying Automation to Work* (Boston, MA: Harvard Business Review Press, 2018).

10. Bob Trebilcock, "NextGen Supply Chain at DHL," Modern Materials Handling, March 3, 2018, https://www.mmh.com/article/next_gen_supply_chain_at_dhl.

11. Vishnu Rajamanickam, "JD.com Opens Automated Warehouse That Employs Four People but Fulfills 200,000 Packages Daily," Freight Waves, June 25, 2018, https://www.freightwaves.com/news/technology/jdcom-opens-automated -warehouse-that-employs-four-people-but-fulfills-200000-packages-daily.

Chapter 3

1. Joe Gardyasz, "Iowa Manufacturers Pivot Quickly to Produce PPE for Health-Care Workers," *Innovation Iowa Magazine*, May 21, 2020, https://innovationia .com/2020/05/21/iowa-manufacturers-pivot-quickly-to-produce-ppe-for-health -care-workers/.

2. Michelle Mark, "An American Factory Owner Who Pivoted to Making Face Shields in 8 Days Has 3 Steps Others Can Follow to Transform Their Factories," *Business Insider*, April 9, 2020, https://www.businessinsider.com/how-us-factories -can-pivot-to-make-ppe-2020-4.

3. "How Businesses Are Pivoting to Make PPE for Front-Line Workers," NBC San Diego, April 10, 2020,://www.nbcsandiego.com/lx/how-businesses-are-pivoting -to-make-ppe-for-front-line-workers/2308006/.

4. "Pivot Power—How GM and Hitachi Moved from Autos to Medical Masks in Six Days," Hitachi, accessed April 9, 2021, https://social-innovation.hitachi /en-us/case_studies/pivot-power-gm-hitachi/.

5. "Renfro CEO: Pivot to PPE Prevented Furloughs, Proved Versatility," Surry County Economic Development Partnership, August 28, 2020, https://www .surryedp.com/renfro-ceo-pivot-to-ppe-prevented-furloughs-proved-versatility/.

6. Eric Volkman, "Kroger to Accept Furloughed Sysco Employees as Temporary Workers," The Motley Fool, March 30, 2020, https://www.fool.com/investing /2020/03/30/kroger-to-accept-furloughed-sysco-employees-as-tem.aspx.

7. Joe Gardyasz, "Iowa Manufacturers Pivot Quickly to Produce PPE for Health-Care Workers," innovationIOWA, May 21, 2020, https://innovationia.com /2020/05/21/iowa-manufacturers-pivot-quickly-to-produce-ppe-for-health-care -workers/.

8. Sameer Hasija, V. "Paddy" Padmanabhan, and Prashant Rampal, "Will the Pandemic Push Knowledge Work into the Gig Economy?," *Harvard Business Review*, June 1, 2020, https://hbr.org/2020/06/will-the-pandemic-push -knowledge-work-into-the-gig-economy.

9. Patricia Cohen, "This Plan Pays to Avoid Layoffs. Why Don't More Employers Use It?," *New York Times*, August 20, 2020, https://www.nytimes.com/2020/08/20/business/economy/jobs-work-sharing-unemployment.html.

10. Melanie Gilarsky, Ryan Nunn, and Jana Parsons, "What Is Work Sharing and How Can It Help the Labor Market?," *Brookings*, April 16, 2020, https://www.brookings.edu/blog/up-front/2020/04/16/what-is-work-sharing-and-how-can-it-help-the-labor-market/.

11. Eric Davis, "i4cp's Talent Ecosystem Integration Model," Institute for Corporate Productivity (i4cp), December 17, 2019, https://www.i4cp.com/infographics/infographic-building-agile-talent-ecosystems.

12. Natalia Peart, "Four HR Officers Create a Solution to Connect People to Work," *Forbes Magazine*, December 9, 2020, https://www.forbes.com/sites/nataliapeart/2020/12/09/four-hr-officers-create-a-solution-to-connect-people-to-work/.

13. John W. Boudreau, Ravin Jesuthasan, and David Creelman, *Lead the Work* (Hoboken, NJ: John Wiley & Sons, 2015).

Chapter 4

1. "Computer and Information Technology Occupations," U.S. Bureau of Labor Statistics, May 14, 2021, https://www.bls.gov/ooh/computer-and-information-technology/home.htm.

2. Ginni Rometty, "We Need to Fill 'New Collar' Jobs That Employers Demand: IBM's Rometty," *USA Today*, December 13, 2016, https://www.usatoday.com/story/tech/columnist/2016/12/13/we-need-fill-new-collar-jobs-employers-demand-ibms-rometty/95382248/.

3. "Make It," CNBC, March 2, 2016, https://www.cnbc.com/make-it/.

4. "IBM News Room," accessed June 26, 2021, https://www-03.ibm.com/press/us/en/pressrelease/52552.wss.

5. Rodney Petersen, Danielle Santos, Matthew C. Smith, Karen A. Wetzel, and Greg Witte, "Workforce Framework for Cybersecurity (NICE Framework)," National Institute of Standards and Technology, https://nvlpubs.nist.gov/nistpubs/SpecialPublications/NIST.SP.800-181r1.pdf.

6. "16 More Industry Leaders Commit to Principles to Grow the Nation's Cybersecurity Workforce—the Aspen Institute," February 26, 2020, https://www.aspeninstitute.org/news/press-release/growing-cybersecurity-workforce/.

7. Quoted in Thomas Bailey and Clive R. Belfield, "Stackable Credentials: Awards for the Future?," Working paper no. 92, Columbia University Community College Research Center, 2017, https://ccrc.tc.columbia.edu/publications /stackable-credentials-awards-for-future.html.

8. Bailey and Belfield, "Stackable Credentials."

9. Bailey and Belfield, "Stackable Credentials."

10. Rachel Vilsack, "Workforce Update: Workers without a College Degree Are Disproportionately Impacted by Covid-19 Job Losses," National Skills Coalition, July 9, 2020. https://www.nationalskillscoalition.org/blog/higher-education/workforce -update-workers-without-a-college-degree-are-disproportionately-impacted-by -covid-19-job-losses/.

11. "Military Crosswalk Search," O*Net Online, accessed April 9, 2021, https:// www.onetonline.org/crosswalk/MOC?b=A&s=leader&g=Go.

12. "The Reskilling Revolution: Better Skills, Better Jobs, Better Education for a Billion People by 2030," World Economic Forum, January 22, 2020, https:// www.weforum.org/press/2020/01/the-reskilling-revolution-better-skills-better -jobs-better-education-for-a-billion-people-by-2030.

13. Kyle Demaria, Kyle Fee, and Keith Wardrip, "Exploring a Skills-Based Approach to Occupational Mobility," 2020, Federal Reserve Bank of Philadelphia and Federal Reserve Bank of Cleveland, https://www.philadelphiafed.org/-/media /frbp/assets/community-development/reports/skills-based-mobility.pdf?la=en.

14. "Occupational Mobility Explorer," accessed June 26, 2021, https://www .philadelphiafed.org/surveys-and-data/community-development-data/occu pational-mobility-explorer.

15. Kate Whiting, "This Is How AI Can Unlock Hidden Talent in the Workplace," accessed June 26, 2021, https://www.weforum.org/agenda/2021/06/jobs -work-skills-future-automation-ai/.

16. Jill Larsen, "At Cisco, We're Trying to Create Our Own 'Gig Economy' for Employees," Ere, May 19, 2017, https://www.ere.net/at-cisco-were-trying-to -create-our-own-gig-economy-for-employees/.

17. "EmPath," accessed April 9, 2021, https://www.empath.net/.

Chapter 5

1. Yaarit Silverstone, Himanshu Tambe, and Susan M. Cantrell, "HR Drives the Agile Organization," Accenture, accessed April 9, 2021, https://www.accenture.com/t20160913T220140__w__/us-en/_acnmedia/Accenture/Conversion-Assets/DotCom/Documents/Global/PDF/Strategy_3/Accenture-Future-of-HR-Trends-Agile-Organizations.pdf.

2. Morgan R. Frank, David Autor, James E. Bessen, Erik Brynjolfsson, Manuel Cebrian, David J. Deming, Maryann Feldman, Matthew Groh, José Lobo, Esteban Moro, Dashun Wang, Hyejin Youn, and Iyad Rahwan, "Toward Understanding the Impact of Artificial Intelligence on Labor," *Proceedings of the National Academy of Sciences* 116, no. 14 (April 2019): 6531–6539, https://doi.org/10.1073/pnas.1900949116.

3. Kevin Kelly, *The Inevitable: Understanding the 12 Technological Forces That Will Shape Our Future* (New York: Penguin Press, 2017).

4. Kelly, *The Inevitable*.

5. Arthur Yeung and Dave Ulrich, *Reinventing the Organization: How Companies Can Deliver Radically Greater Value in Fast-Changing Markets* (Boston, MA: Harvard Business Review Press, 2019).

6. "Holacracy," accessed April 9, 2021, https://www.holacracy.org/.

7. Gary Hamel and Michele Zanini, *Humanocracy: Creating Organizations as Amazing as the People inside Them* (Boston, MA: Harvard Business Review Press, 2020).

8. Ravin Jesuthasan, "Metrics for the Future of Work," HR Tech Outlook, accessed April 9, 2021,, https://hr-analytics.hrtechoutlook.com/cxoinsights/metrics-for-the-future-of-work-nid-765.html.

Chapter 6

1. John W. Boudreau and Pete Ramstad, "COVID's Hidden Promise: Future Work Design is Agile Innovation," LinkedIn, February 9, 2021, https://www.linkedin.com/pulse/covids-hidden-promise-future-work-design-agile-john-boudreau/.

2. Boudreau and Ramstad, "COVID's Hidden Promise."

3. John W. Boudreau, *Retooling HR: Using Proven Business Tools to Make Better Decisions about Talent* (Boston, MA: Harvard Business Review Press, 2014).

4. Mike Walsh, "When Algorithms Make Managers Worse," *Harvard Business Review*, May 8, 2019, https://hbr.org/2019/05/when-algorithms-make-managers -worse.

5. John W. Boudreau, Carolyn Lavelle Rearick, and Ian Ziskin, *Black Holes and White Spaces: Reimagining the Future of Work and HR with the CHREATE Project* (Alexandria, VA: Society for Human Resources Management, 2018).

6. Antonio Zappulla, "The Future of Business? Purpose, Not Just Profit," World Economic Forum, January 17 2019, https://www.weforum.org/agenda/2019/01 /why-businesses-must-be-driven-by-purpose-as-well-as-profits/.

7. "HR4.0: Shaping People Strategies in the Fourth Industrial Revolution," World Economic Forum, December 2019, http://www3.weforum.org/docs/WEF_NES_ Whitepaper_HR4.0.pdf.

8. "An Exciting New Normal for Flexible Working," Unilever, June 23, 2020, https://www.unilever.com/news/news-and-features/Feature-article/2020/an -exciting-new-normal-for-flexible-working.html.

9. "Understanding and Measuring Job Quality, Part 2: Indicators of Job Quality," Chartered Institute of Personnel and Development (CIPD), January 8, 2018, 4, https://www.cipd.co.uk/knowledge/work/job-quality-value-creation/measuring -job-quality-report.

10. "Mutual Gains Approach," Wikipedia, April 14, 2018, http://en.wikipedia .org/w/index.php?title=Mutual_Gains_Approach&oldid=836449404.

11. John W. Boudreau and Jonathan Donner, "Are You Ready to Lead Work without Jobs?," *Sloan Management Review*, April 8, 2021, https://sloanreview.mit .edu/article/are-you-ready-to-lead-work-without-jobs/.

12. Ravin Jesuthasan and John W. Boudreau, *Reinventing Jobs: A 4-Step Approach for Applying Automation to Work* (Boston, MA: Harvard Business Review Press, 2018).

13. Robert Goffee and Gareth Jones, *Why Should Anyone Be Led by You?: What It Takes to Be an Authentic Leader* (Boston, MA: Harvard Business Review Press, 2006).

14. John W. Boudreau and Jonathan Donner, "Are You Ready to Lead Work without Jobs?"

Chapter 7

1. John W. Boudreau, "Work in the Future Will Fall into These 4 Categories," *Harvard Business Review*, March 17, 2016, https://hbr.org/2016/03/work-in-the -future-will-fall-into-these-4-categories.

2. Joseph Fuller, Manjari Raman, Allison Bailey, and Nithya Vaduganathan, "Rethinking the On-Demand Workforce," *Harvard Business Review*, November 1, 2020, https://hbr.org/2020/11/rethinking-the-on-demand-workforce.

3. "The Promise of Platform Work: Understanding the Ecosystem," World Economic Forum, January 2020, http://www3.weforum.org/docs/WEF_The_Promise _of_Platform_Work.pdf.

4. Wayne F. Cascio and John W. Boudreau, "Talent Management of Nonstandard Employees," in *The Oxford Handbook of Talent Management*, ed. David G. Collings, Kamel Mellahi, and Wayne F. Cascio (Oxford, UK: Oxford University Press, 2017), 494–520.

5. Christa L. Wilkin, "I Can't Get No Job Satisfaction: Meta-Analysis Comparing Permanent and Contingent Workers," *Journal of Organizational Behavior* 34, no. 1 (2013): 47–64, https://onlinelibrary.wiley.com/doi/abs/10.1002/job.1790.

6. Michael Clinton, Claudia Bernhard-Oettel, Thomas Rigotti, and Jeroen de Jong, "Expanding the Temporal Context of Research on Non-Ppermanent Work: Previous Experience, Duration of and Time Remaining on Contracts and Employment Continuity Expectations." *Career Development International* 16, no. 2 (2011): 114–139, https://doi.org/10.1108/13620431111115596.

7. Lydia Aletraris, "How Satisfied Are They and Why? A Study of Job Satisfaction, Job Rewards, Gender and Temporary Agency Workers in Australia," *Human Relations: Studies towards the Integration of the Social Sciences* 63, no. 8 (2010): 1129–1155, https://doi.org/10.1177/0018726709354131.

8. Peter Allan and Stephen Seinko, "A Comparison of Contingent and Core Workers' Perceptions of Their Jobs' Characteristics and Motivational Properties," *S. A. M. Advanced Management Journal* 62, no. 3 (1997): 4–9.

9. Joseph P. Broschak and Alison Davis-Blake, "Mixing Standard Work and Nonstandard Deals: The Consequences of Heterogeneity in Employment Arrangements," *Academy of Management Journal* 49, no. 2 (2006): 371–393, https://doi.org /10.5465/amj.2006.20786085.

10. John W. Boudreau and Robert Cross, "Are Freelancers Your Best Performers? Applying ONA to the Gig Economy," Visier, May 8, 2018, https://www.visier.com /clarity/freelancers-best-performers-organizational-network-analysis-gig-economy.

11. This section based on Boudreau and Cross, "Are Freelancers Your Best Performers?"

12. "Organizational Network Analysis," Wikipedia, January 21, 2021, https:// en.wikipedia.org/w/index.php?title=Organizational_network_analysis&oldid =1001831977.

13. "What Is Organizational Network Analysis (ONA)?," Rob Cross, February 16, 2020, https://www.robcross.org/what-is-organizational-network-analysis/.

14. Rob Cross and Robert J. Thomas, "A Smarter Way to Network," *Harvard Business Review*, July–August 2011, https://hbr.org/2011/07/managing-yourself -a-smarter-way-to-network.

15. Rob Cross, Rob, Tina Opie, Greg Pryor, and Keith Rollag, "Connect and Adapt," *Organizational Dynamics* 47, no. 2 (2018): 115–123, https://doi.org/10 .1016/j.orgdyn.2017.08.003.

16. John W. Boudreau, "New Ways of Getting Work Require a Common Language of Work," CFO, March 25, 2015, https://www.cfo.com/people/2015/03 /in-a-new-era-of-work-skills-are-lost-in-translation-failure-to-communicate/.

17. "7 Ways the Private Sector Can Contribute to Universal Health Coverage," World Economic Forum, September 20, 2019, https://www.weforum.org/agenda /2019/09/7-ways-the-private-sector-can-contribute-to-universal-health-coverage.

18. "Universal Health Coverage," Worldbank, accessed April 10, 2021, https:// www.worldbank.org/en/topic/universalhealthcoverage.

19. "The Promise of Platform Work: Understanding the Ecosystem," World Economic Forum, January 2020, 12, http://www3.weforum.org/docs/WEF _The_Promise_of_Platform_Work.pdf; Karolien Lenaerts, Willem Pieter De Groen, Zachary Kilhoffer, Romain Bosc, and Nicolas Salez, "Online Talent Platforms, Labour Market Intermediaries and the Changing World of Work," CEPS, May 16, 2018, https://www.ceps.eu/ceps-publications/online-talent-platforms-labour -market-intermediaries-and-changing-world-work/.

20. Chris Forde, Mark Stuart, Simon Joyce, Liz Oliver, Danat Valizade, Gabriella Alberti, Kate Hardy, Vera Trappmann, Charles Umney, and Calum Carson,

"The Social Protection of Workers in the Platform Economy," European Parliament, December 7, 2017, 11, https://www.europarl.europa.eu/thinktank/en/document.html?reference=IPOL_STU(2017)614184.

21. Andrew Boozary, "Universal Health Care: The Affordable Dream," *Harvard Public Health Review*, April 16, 2015, http://harvardpublichealthreview.org/universal-health-care-the-affordable-dream/.

22. "Universal Basic Income," Wikipedia, April 6, 2021, https://en.wikipedia.org/w/index.php?title=Universal_basic_income&oldid=1016400831.

23. "Andrew Yang for Mayor of NYC: Forward New York," Yang2020, accessed April 10, 2021, https://www.yang2020.com/what-is-freedom-dividend-faq/.

24. Guy Standing, "Coronavirus Has Made Basic Income Not Just Desirable but Vital," World Economic Forum, April 13, 2020, https://www.weforum.org/agenda/2020/04/coronavirus-made-basic-income-vital/.

25. Vili Lehdonvirta, "Could Universal Basic Income Counter the Gig Economy's Problems?," Oxford Internet Institute, April 13, 2017, https://ilabour.oii.ox.ac.uk/could-universal-basic-income-counter-the-gig-economys-problems/.

26. The World Bank, "Protecting People and Economies: Integrated Policy Responses to COVID-19," The World Bank, May 17, 2020, 13, https://openknowledge.worldbank.org/handle/10986/33770.

27. Sarah Holder, "2021 Will Be the Year of Guaranteed Income Experiments," Bloomberg CityLab, January 4, 2021, https://www.bloomberg.com/news/articles/2021-01-04/guaranteed-income-gains-popularity-after-covid-19.

28. Heather Somerville, "Seattle Passes Law Letting Uber, Lyft Drivers Unionize," Reuters, December 14, 2015, https://www.reuters.com/article/us-washington-uber/seattle-passes-law-letting-uber-lyft-drivers-unionize-idUSKBN0TX2NO20151215.

29. US Chamber of Commerce, "U.S. Chamber Files Lawsuit Challenging Seattle's Drivers' Union Ordinance," March 3, 2016, https://www.uschamber.com/press-release/us-chamber-files-lawsuit-challenging-seattle-s-drivers-union-ordinance.

30. Daniel Weissner, "U.S. Court Revives Challenge to Seattle's Uber, Lyft Union Law," Reuters, May 11, 2018, https://www.reuters.com/article/us-uber-seattle-unions-idUSKBN1IC27C.

31. Kurt Vandaele, "Will Trade Unions Survive in the Platform Economy? Emerging Patterns of Platform Workers' Collective Voice and Representation

in Europe," Working paper, European Trade Union Institute, 2018, 6, accessed April 10, 2021, https://www.etui.org/publications/working-papers/will-trade -unions-survive-in-the-platform-economy-emerging-patterns-of-platform -workers-collective-voice-and-representation-in-europe.

32. Vandaele, "Will Trade Unions Survive in the Platform Economy?"

33. John W. Boudreau, "Are Unions Tomorrow's Work Platforms?," Visier, September 25, 2018, https://www.visier.com/clarity/are-unions-tomorrows-work -platforms/.

34. "STUNT & SAFETY 2014 TV/Theatrical Contracts Digest," Sag-Aftra, accessed April 9, 2021, https://www.sagaftra.org/files/stunt_safety_digest_2014.pdf.

35. Adam Davidson, "What Hollywood Can Teach Us about the Future of Work," *New York Times*, May 5, 2015, https://www.nytimes.com/2015/05/10 /magazine/what-hollywood-can-teach-us-about-the-future-of-work.html.

36. "CAPS Payroll," accessed April 10, 2021, https://www.capspayroll.com/.

37. John Marcus, "More Students Are 'Stacking' Credentials en Route to a Degree," *Wired*, June 2, 2020, https://www.wired.com/story/students-stacking -credentials-route-degree/.

38. "Persistence & Retention: 2019," National Student Clearinghouse Research Center, July 10, 2019, https://nscresearchcenter.org/snapshotreport35-first-year -persistence-and-retention/.

39. "Completing College: 2019 National Report," National Student Clearinghouse Research Center, December 2019, https://nscresearchcenter.org/wp-con tent/uploads/Completions_Report_2019.pdf.

40. Evelyn Ganzglass, "Scaling 'Stackable Credentials,'" Center for Postsecondary and Economic Success at the Center for Law and Social Policy (CLASP), March 2014, 7–8, https://www.clasp.org/sites/default/files/public/resources-and -publications/files/2014-03-21-Stackable-Credentials-Paper-FINAL.pdf.

41. Lynda Gratton and Andrew Scott, *The 100-Year Life: Living and Working in an Age of Longevity* (London, England: Bloomsbury Business, 2017), http://www .100yearlife.com/the-book/.

42. Jeff Schwartz, Kelly Monahan, Steve Hatfield, and Siri Anderson, "No Time to Retire: Redesigning Work for our Aging Workforce," Deloitte, December 7, 2018, https://www2.deloitte.com/us/en/insights/focus/technology-and-the-future-of -work/redesigning-work-for-our-aging-workforce.html.

43. "Are We All Becoming Freelancers?," SwissLife, June 6, 2017, https://www
.swisslife.com/en/home/hub/are-we-all-becoming-freelancers.html.

Conclusions and Next Steps

1. Kari Naimon, "Deconstruct to Reconstruct How Providence Health System
Built an Internal Talent Marketplace," Institute for Corporate Productivity (i4cp),
February 10, 2021, https://www.i4cp.com/productivity-blog/deconstruct-to
-reconstruct-how-providence-health-system-built-an-internal-talent-marketplace.

2. Emily DeCiccio, "'Planning is the Antidote to Panic': Providence Hospital
System Defies America's Slow Vaccine Rollout Trend," CNBC, January 4, 2021,
https://www.cnbc.com/2021/01/04/providence-hospital-system-defies-americas
-slow-vaccine-rollout-trend.html.

Index